PASSION FOR YOUR NAME

'As a genuine and sincere worshipper, and one gifted with words and melodies to express it, Tim Hughes takes seriously what he does, and how and why he does it. To read this book is to share in a journey of discovery, of truths encountered, principles gleaned, mistakes made and lessons learned. A valuable companion for all worshippers, especially those seeking to lead others in a manner that is pleasing to God.'

Graham Kendrick

'So many of Tim's songs convey important truths in a beautiful way. And the good news is, his book does exactly the same. Written from the heart, *Passion for Your Name* is full of timely and timeless advice for today's worship leader.'

Matt Redman

Passion for Your Name

TIM HUGHES

survivor

ISBN 1 84291 175 9

Published by
KINGSWAY COMMUNICATIONS LTD
Lottbridge Drove, Eastbourne BN23 6NT, England.
Email: books@kingsway.co.uk

Book design and production for the publishers by
Bookprint Creative Services, P.O. Box 827, BN21 3YJ, England.
Printed in United States.

Dedication

Mum, Dad, Pete, Bee and Steve, for always loving me. I can't imagine life without you all.

Mike Pilavachi, for your friendship, encouragement and loyalty. Your generosity and support amaze me. I love you very much.

Contents

Acknowledgements

I'm very grateful to all those who read through the manuscript and made some extremely helpful suggestions. Thank you Mike Pilavachi (your comments particularly made a huge difference to this book), Peter Hughes, Stephen Hughes, Jonny Hughes, Chris Bullivant and Ali MacInnes.

Thanks to Rachel Harper for reading through the manuscript. Thank you especially for being there and for your friendship. I appreciate you so much.

Thanks to Matt, Beth, Maisey and Noah. You've taught me so much about worship and living it out. Thanks for cheering me on. It means so much.

Thanks to the Greigs: Bill III, Rhonnie, Bill, Taylor and David, for letting me stay with you in Ventura. Your hospitality and friendship are such a blessing.

Thanks to Les Moir for your support and input both personally and with this project.

Thanks to all the guys at Kingsway/Survivor for

putting so much work into this book. To John Pac, Richard Herkes, Carolyn Owen, Dave Roberts and Georgina Earey.

Finally thank you to all my friends, family and work colleagues at Soul Survivor. I've learnt so much about God's amazing love and grace through hanging out with you all.

Foreword

This book is a fantastic resource for anyone who is passionate about the worship of God but especially for worship leaders, pastors and musicians. In these days when worship with music has become so central in the life of the church, and indeed worship leaders can sometimes be treated as celebrities, this book is both timely and prophetic.

Tim eloquently reminds us what worship is all about. The sections that deal with heart attitudes are vital if we are not to lose our way and turn worship into an industry that is personality driven and consumer sensitive. Indeed, one of the messages of this book is that worship should only be driven by Jesus' personality and should be Holy Spirit sensitive! We must not lose the plot. There is room for only one star of the show, one celebrity, one hero in the Christian faith and his name is Jesus. As Revelation chapters 4 and 5 so graphically illustrate, the four living creatures, 24 elders, 10,000 times 10,000 angels and every creature in heaven and on earth and under the earth and on the sea (we come in there somewhere) are but the supporting cast, the appreciative audience. At the centre stands the Lion of the tribe of Judah who appears as a lamb who has been slain. What an amazing picture! It is this vision of Jesus' role and our roles that shines through again and again in the pages of this book.

While *Passion for Your Name* is great applied theology, it is also intensely practical. Tim writes to serve other worship leaders and musicians. He writes of these things only as one who has thought deeply about the issues, not in an ivory tower but from the perspective of having to lead worship week in week out in a local church setting as well as at events throughout the world. The chapters on leading a band, choosing a song list, musical dynamics and practical tips are worth their weight in gold. I hope many pastors and leaders will read this book – the principles and the practice here will transform the worship of any church. This is honestly the best practical book on worship I have read.

The integrity of a book like this rests on the character of the author. So a word about Tim. I have known Tim since he was eleven, and the past few years he has been my colleague and ministry partner at Soul Survivor. We have travelled the world together and had the privilege of meeting some amazing men and women of God and seeing God do some wonderful things. Tim lives it out like no one I know. His humility, modesty and servant heart constantly amaze and challenge me. Now his songs are being sung around the world, he is exactly the same person I have always known. He is a pastor's delight. He is a team player. There is no ego. This book is real because Tim is real. He has a passion for the whole church and a heart to serve and release other worship leaders into their calling. As you may have guessed, I am extremely proud of him!

I wholeheartedly commend *Passion for Your Name* to you. Not only is there great biblical teaching and very practical and helpful hints here, but it also draws you to Jesus, the object and centre of our worship.

Mike Pilavachi
Soul Survivor

1

One Thing

I t was a hot and humid Sunday morning. Sweat was pouring down my face and the service hadn't even begun. The congregation was gathering, but as I looked to the front of the church I was perplexed to see no drums, no amps, no keyboards. There weren't even any microphones or speakers set up. I wondered how on earth we were going to worship. And then it began. A loud voice pierced the silence and instantly all the people were on their feet singing their hearts out. The harmonies and melodies that filled the air created the most beautiful sound. The joy and heartfelt adoration on the faces of the congregation was infectious. I wanted what they had.

Here were people wholeheartedly consumed with their Saviour. They had a joy and contentment that made me envious. Yet when I looked at their surroundings I was confused. The church of the Prince of Peace is based in the township of Inanda, Durban, South Africa.

The people of this township live in extreme poverty. AIDS is rife, and pain and suffering are part of everyday life. Surely their songs should be those of lament and pain, not joy and celebration? It took a while to sink in, but as the service progressed the reason for their joy struck me. They had encountered the Lord Jesus. They knew where they had come from; they were well aware of their present, but ultimately they understood where they were going. They understood completely that Jesus was enough. Whatever life threw at them, it couldn't rob them of the glorious riches of knowing God and being known by him. They would always have reason to praise. That Sunday morning I learned an invaluable lesson about worship. Worship is not about songs or music. Worship is all about Jesus.

Watching before working

In the West we are so driven and ambitious. Everything is about getting results and making things happen. The primary focus is on gifting – if you're clever then you'll achieve; if you're beautiful then you'll be favoured. As humans we have become self-obsessed. Every day we live to impress others and earn respect. The gospel, however, turns this way of life on its head. Until we surrender our rights and die to ourselves we can achieve nothing. As Jesus said, 'Whoever finds his life will lose it, and whoever loses his life for my sake will find it' (Matthew 10:39). The beauty of the gospel is that we cannot earn our salvation. We could work for ever and a day and still never earn a moment of God's grace. The first thing God calls us to do is to watch him, to gaze into his eyes and behold his greatness.

My family had a tradition that I hated. Regularly we would have guests round for Sunday lunch. After the meal my two brothers and I would clear away and wash up, while my parents and the guests would sit down for coffee. Every Sunday without fail one of my brothers would seem to desperately need the toilet after the meal. Apparently, he couldn't wait, so while we washed and dried the dishes, that brother would sit on the toilet. This always wound me up, but the thing that made me cross was when he would wander through with a really smug look on his face just as we were about to finish. Perhaps it's because of these Sunday afternoons that I can relate to Mary and Martha's encounter with Jesus!

> As Jesus and his disciples were on their way, he came to a village where a woman named Martha opened her home to him. She had a sister called Mary, who sat at the Lord's feet listening to what he said. But Martha was distracted by all the preparations that had to be made. She came to him and asked, 'Lord, don't you care that my sister has left me to do the work by myself? Tell her to help me!' 'Martha, Martha,' the Lord answered, 'you are worried and upset about many things, but only one thing is needed. Mary has chosen what is better, and it will not be taken away from her.' (Luke 10:38–42)

It's not every day that the Saviour of the world pops in for tea. Mary and Martha must have been very excited. Straightaway Martha swings into action and exerts herself in all the preparations at hand. While she's rushing around doing all the work, her sister Mary just sits at Jesus' feet hanging on his every word. Surely Mary is in the wrong here. Isn't she being selfish and lazy? Eventually Martha loses her cool and turns to Jesus for help. Her question is brilliantly crafted and deserving of all the sympathy and respect in the world: 'Lord, don't you care that my sister has left me to do the work by myself?'

The answer she received must have taken her by surprise. Jesus tenderly points out that Martha has missed the point. The key word in this passage is 'distracted': 'But Martha was distracted by all the preparations that had to be made.' Martha thought she was doing the right and honourable thing. There was work to be done and she was going to do it. By working hard, she would demonstrate to Jesus how much she loved him. However, this was not what Jesus desired from her. He desired Martha's intimacy – her company. In this short story, it was Mary who chose the right thing – the one thing that was needed. She sat at Jesus' feet and enjoyed spending time with him, learning from him and discovering more about him. Jesus was delighted by this response. Mary chose to watch before she chose to work.

As worship leaders we must take note of this lesson. We are very good at doing things – organising meetings, planning services and attending prayer meetings. All these are important and worthy, but they must never come at the expense of knowing God. Recently I had a few days to spend time with the Lord. I was so excited about this chance to escape and spend some quality time alone, but as I sat down on the first morning I was surprised at how hard I found it to settle. My mind kept buzzing around with all the things I had to do, and I would put off reading and praying by finding other tasks I felt were more important. After a while I realised that, like Martha, I was becoming 'distracted' by things of lesser importance. Eventually I managed to still myself and was refreshed as I sat at Jesus' feet.

Before we play our songs, before we commit to serving Jesus, we need to adore and cherish him. Sometimes amid the pressure to succeed we lose this focus. A passage of Scripture that expresses beautifully the heart of a radical worshipper is found in Psalm 27:4: 'One thing I ask of the Lord, this is what I seek: that I may dwell in the house of the Lord all the days of my life, to gaze upon the beauty of the Lord and to seek him in his temple.'

If you are involved in leading worship or playing in a worship team, the most important thing you can do to be effective in your ministry is to seek after God, to chase after a glimpse of his glory. Desire this first, before you learn to grow in your musicality and leadership skills.

Highest calling

Worship is our highest calling. There is nothing in this life that we can do of more importance. On this theme, John Piper says:

Missions is not the ultimate goal of the church. Worship is. Mission exists because worship doesn't. Worship is ultimate, not missions, because God is ultimate, not man. When the age is over, and countless millions of the redeemed fall on their faces before the throne of God, missions will be no more. It is a temporary necessity. But worship abides for ever.[1]

When that day comes, and we behold the Lord in all his glory, we will worship and praise him for ever. That is what we have been created for. We have been designed by God for this sole purpose. It is our duty and joy to worship God. In Matthew's Gospel, Jesus responded to the question 'Teacher, which is the greatest commandment in the Law?' by saying, 'Love the Lord your God with all your heart and with all your soul and with all your mind. This is the first and greatest commandment' (Matthew 22:37). This is why Jesus rejoiced so in Mary's response to him. She didn't give her offerings of preparing food or gifts; she gave all she had – herself. This is the worship that Jesus requires. Singing songs to God isn't enough; that in itself is not worship. Worship involves offering to God all that we are and all that we'll be; offering our heart, soul and mind.

In his letter to the Romans, Paul says, 'Therefore, I urge you, brothers, in view of God's mercy, to offer your bodies as living sacrifices, holy and pleasing to God – this is your spiritual act of worship' (Romans 12:1). We must remind ourselves that worship is our all-consuming response to God. It affects the way we live. When we live life in the knowledge that all we do is worship, we change.

For three years I studied history at Sheffield University. I have to be honest and say that I found my studies pretty boring. I was not the most enthusiastic member of my class. However, I remember being really challenged by a verse in 1 Corinthians that says, 'So whether you eat or drink or whatever you do, do it all for the glory of God' (10:31). It dawned on me that when writing an essay I should be doing it to the glory of God. Even something as dull and boring as a history essay can be an act of worship. In fact all that we do should be to the glory of God – our words, deeds and choices. For this reason worship also involves serving and loving others.

When Jesus talked about the greatest commandment, he then moved on to talk about the second commandment, which is like the first: 'Love your neighbour as yourself' (Matthew 22:37). We first worship the Lord and then from that place we look to love those around us. We cannot worship if we don't also serve.

Overflow

Worship pours from the overflow of our hearts. If you squeeze an orange, out of it will come orange juice. If you were to have your heart squeezed, what would flow out? Would it be a love for yourself? Would it be your love for a pop band, a football team, a girlfriend or boyfriend? Would it be your passion for Jesus? We all worship. Humans have been created to worship. The big question is: who or what will we worship? John Wimber once said, 'Our heart's desire should be to worship God;

we have been designed by God for this purpose. If we don't worship God, we'll worship something or someone else.' If Jesus isn't the number one priority in our lives, we will never fully worship him. We certainly won't be moved to share the love of Jesus with others.

A while back I was on a plane heading to Los Angeles. As I sat there trying to keep myself amused, I noticed that a few rows in front of me was Chris Martin, the lead singer of the band Coldplay. I have to admit I was star struck. I watched everything he did: how he ate his croissant, how he talked to the cabin crew and how he listened to his Walkman. As soon as I was off the plane I was telling all my friends about this amazing encounter. I'm embarrassed to say that I got quite carried away. My eyes had seen someone famous and I wanted the world to know.

When our eyes truly see Jesus and our hearts comprehend his life-changing love, we will not be able to contain ourselves from telling others about him. It will be bursting within us. I've sat in so many meetings where we've been exhorted to get out there and tell the world about Jesus; to go and serve; to demonstrate the love of God. However, if we spend our day caring for others, meeting people's needs and serving communities purely because of guilt, we will be far less effective than if we go out and serve because we are so in love with Jesus – then we could see the world changed.

Jesus has to be at the centre of our worship. When Mother Teresa was asked how she went about each day she said, 'Each morning I meditate on Jesus. I then go and look for him in disguise.' This is how we should worship. We first look to Jesus, and then we look to love him among the poor and broken. As Bishop Graham Cray said, 'Worship without mission is self-indulgent. Mission without worship is self-defeating.' [2]

If our worship and adoration of Jesus doesn't lead us to the poor or into the streets, then it's purely self-indulgent. On the other hand, if we try and reach the world in our own strength we will see little fruit. Our love for others and desire to serve has to come from our overwhelming love for Jesus. True worship means that in everything we do, we do it for Jesus.

> You call us first to love Your name,
> To worship You.
> To please Your heart our one desire,
> O Lord.
>
> *If there's one thing we are called to do,*
> *It's to love You, to adore You.*
> *We will bring our all and worship You,*
> *Bow before You, as we love You.*
>
> Your honour, Lord, Your name's renown
> We long to see.
> So let the glory of Your name
> Be praised. [3]

Notes

1. John Piper, *Let the Nations be Glad: The Supremacy of God in Missions* (Baker Books, 1993), p. 11.
2. Graham Cray, from his seminar 'Worship and

Worship Songs – a Theological Reflection', December 2002.
3. 'If there's one thing', Tim Hughes, Thankyou Music, 2001.

2

Shape of My Heart

Recently I attended a Christian awards ceremony in America, and it was quite a surreal experience. Turning up to the event, people paraded around in their best tuxedos and dresses. I kept thinking that this must be what the Oscars feel like. Throughout the night many different awards were given out, including best album, best male and female artist and best song. Many tears were shed as people gave speeches, thanking their families, friends, managers, pets and anyone else they could think of. It was quite a shock when my name was announced for one of the awards. The only thought going through my mind as I walked to the front was, 'Tim, don't you dare trip up.' I mumbled some incoherent 'thank you' speech and headed backstage.

It was then that the nightmare really began. First I was ushered into a room where I was greeted by ten photographers who each took my picture. After that I was whisked off to another room, led to the front and left to fend for myself. Before me were about a hundred reporters, who started to bombard me with all sorts of questions. I was so shell-shocked that I had no idea what to say. My answers got more and more unintelligible and confused as I went on, until I started talking rubbish. It wasn't long before the questions dried up. Having no clue what to do I stood there for a few moments. There was a very embarrassed silence. All I could think to do was say, 'See you,' and walk out. It definitely won't go down as one of the cool moments in my life.

In many ways worship music has become an industry. Many predict that in the coming years it will become the dominant genre in Christian music worldwide. There has been an explosion in the number of songs, CDs, DVDs, websites and books that are now dedicated to this worship movement. I think it's wonderful to see such a release of creativity; the wealth of resources can only be a blessing to the church. However, in the midst of all that's happening, I sometimes feel a bit uncomfortable. As worship leaders, are we getting too preoccupied with the sounds and songs we are creating? Is there a danger that we look first and foremost at gifting and talents, and forget the key thing: the heart?

John Wimber once said, 'The difficulty will not be so much in the writing of new and great music; the test will be in the godliness of those who deliver it.'[1] It's quite a wake-up call. There can be so many perks to being a worship leader. However, what you see on a Sunday morning is only the tip of the iceberg. Are we willing to allow God to deal with all that is below the surface so that what is visible has integrity? In the long term, who we are when no one is looking has a direct bearing on the fruitfulness of our ministry. Worship is a way of life. How we use our money and possessions, how we relate to our friends and neighbours, how we spend our time and how much of the fruit of the Spirit is evident in our lives, are the most crucial areas we need to be looking at. These issues are so much more important than questions of chord progressions and song selection.

A man after God's heart

My favourite character in the Bible is David. I keep coming back to him again and again. Here is a man who wore his heart on his sleeve. His strengths and flaws were there for all to see. As I've read through David's life I have found five key characteristics that spur me on in the way I live my life. These are traits that I want to pursue.

A heart after God

David is described in many ways throughout the Bible. The phrase that perhaps summarises him best is that he was a 'man after [God's] own heart'. Throughout his life he actively and passionately chased after God. Whether as a simple shepherd boy, a king or a father, he sought the will of God. We often see David enquiring of the Lord. Even though he sometimes failed, he knew the importance of living life God's way, rather than pursuing his own selfish ambition. One striking story is found in 1 Samuel.

David and his men reached Ziklag on the third day. Now the Amalekites had raided the Negev and Ziklag. They had attacked Ziklag and burned it, and had taken captive the women and all who were in it, both young and old. They killed none of them but carried them off as they went on their way. When David and his men came to Ziklag, they found it destroyed by fire and their wives and sons and daughters taken captive. So David and his men wept aloud until they had no strength left to weep. David's two wives had been captured – Ahinoam of Jezreel and Abigail, the widow of Nabal of Carmel. David was greatly distressed because the men were talking of stoning him; each one was bitter in spirit because of his sons and daughters. But David found strength in the Lord his God. Then David said to Abiathar the priest, the son of Ahimelech, 'Bring me the ephod.' Abiathar brought it to him, and David enquired of the Lord, 'Shall I pursue this raiding party? Will I overtake them?' 'Pursue them,' he answered. 'You will certainly overtake them and succeed in the rescue.' (1 Samuel 30:1–8)

David and his men had returned to their base in Ziklag to discover it burned to a crisp with all their children and wives kidnapped. One can hardly begin to imagine the sheer panic and terror that must have fallen upon David. To make everything worse, David's men were so consumed with anger and resentment that they talked of stoning him. In this kind of situation, what would you do? My initial reaction would be to run for my life. I'm not sure I'd have responded the way David did. In the midst of such pressure and pain he found a priest with an unpronounceable name and took time out to enquire of the Lord. Surely this wasn't the time to sit around and pray. Something needed to be done. David chose, however, to concern himself with doing it God's way. He didn't assume that he knew best. He didn't want a good idea; he waited for a God idea.

It is so important for worship leaders to be constantly enquiring of the Lord. We need to be so desperate for God that we'll do whatever it takes to follow him. We will be so much more effective in our ministries if we seek the will of God and do it. This involves spending time with our heavenly Father. We cannot know the heart of God without first being still and listening. For each of us the hidden place with God is crucial. Sadly all too often we let our ministries get in the way of our relationship with God. We become so busy that the noise of the world around us swamps out the voice of the Lord. We find ourselves more focused on doing the work of the Lord than on seeking the Lord of the work.

How did God bring David to the place where in times of crisis he would automatically turn to the Lord? It was in the place of wilderness, in that hidden place, on his own looking after sheep, that God seemed to equip him for the years ahead. These years that could have seemed like wasted years were anything but. In fact they were the most important years. Where did David learn to write his songs? On a hill, in the middle of the night. Where did David write Psalm 23, 'The Lord is my Shepherd'? It wasn't in the palace.

When David prepared to take on the giant Goliath, the people around tried to suggest that, as David was only a boy, he wouldn't have a chance. Look at his immediate reply:

'Your servant has been keeping his father's sheep. When a lion or a bear came and carried off a sheep from the flock, I went after it, struck it and rescued the sheep from its mouth. When it turned on me, I seized it by its hair, struck it and killed it. Your servant has killed both the lion and the bear; this uncircumcised Philistine will be like one of them, because he has defied the armies of the living God.' (1 Samuel 17:34–36)

Wasted years? While he was looking after sheep God was preparing David's heart for all the responsibility and blessing he was to give him. He learned valuable lessons that would form him for the rest of his life.

When I was 14 I learned how to play the guitar. The main reason I wanted to learn was so that I could worship in my room, on my own. Once I'd learned G, C, D and Em I realised that I could play most of the worship songs around – especially after discovering a capo! I would spend hours singing my heart out, driving my family mad. Looking back, I can see how God was deepening my love for him and developing my understanding of him. I learned so much of what worship was about. It was often during those times that I would feel a conviction about a wrong attitude, or at other times of distress I would sense God's peace in a tangible way. God was preparing me and moulding me to be the man he intended me to be. He still is. Those times were so precious, and anyone involved in leading God's people in worship needs to seek those times alone.

If we're not learning how to worship before him on our own, then how can we stand before others and lead them in worship? Andy Park says, 'Worship leading is taking your private cry and making it public.'[2] We cannot lead people to a place where we haven't been ourselves. Like David we need to embrace the hidden place and learn to seek after God's heart.

Humility

Pride is an ugly trait. It always winds me up watching celebrities on TV or reading interviews with people who clearly think that they are God's gift to the human race. We often react against people who are full of themselves, being very quick to pass judgement. But maybe we're not so good at recognising the arrogance in our own hearts. If we're honest with ourselves, the lure of being recognised and being appreciated can be a huge pull on our lives.

I will never forget the first year I led worship at the Soul Survivor festival. It was all quite new to me and to be honest I was rather overwhelmed by it. After one session a young girl came up to me and asked if I might sign her badge seven times. Inside I was ecstatic. I thought, 'I've made it.' However, I remembered that I had to be cool and make it look as if this was an everyday occurrence. So I played it down and suggested that I only sign her badge once. I scribbled my name and a Bible verse. She looked at the name, looked up at me, and then said with a tone that failed to hide her disappointment, 'Oh! Are you not Matt Redman?'

In the context of worship there can only be one star, and that is Jesus. He alone is the famous one. As worship leaders we need to be aware of pride taking root in our hearts. The truth is that often pride is a very subtle thing, but if not addressed it can rule us. We have a responsibility to actively seek humility.

A friend once shared three questions that he would often ask himself. They reveal a lot about your inner self.

1. *How do you handle compliments?* When things go well, does it go to your head? Do you enjoy success too much? Do you feed on the compliments and replay them in your mind?

2. *How do you handle criticisms?* When people suggest that maybe there were too many new songs in that worship set, for example, how do you respond? Do you become defensive and immediately justify yourself, or do you have the humility to take on board what they have said and consider whether they have a point?

3. *How do you deal with your colleagues?* When others are used more in worship than you and people are quick to praise and encourage them, how do you feel? Does jealousy consume you or can you delight in the fact that God is blessing them?

If you know that the whole pride issue is something you struggle with, what can you do? I think the best way to grow in humility is to learn to serve. David had a humble heart and clearly knew what it meant to serve. Looking into his story we see that after he'd been anointed to become the next King of Israel he returned straightaway to tending his flock. If I were told that I was to be the next King of England I would quit my day job and live it up. Not David. He learned to serve God in the hiddenness of looking after sheep, and that humility stayed with him when he was promoted to king.

I was recently challenged by the story of a well-known worship leader who as a young man was very keen to be involved in leading worship. He spoke to his pastor about his desire and this calling on his life, and was offered a job as a cleaner for the church. He thought that he might as well take it, as it wouldn't be long before he was up front leading the church in worship. As time went on and his main role continued to be cleaning the toilets and hoovering the carpets, he started to resent it. He couldn't understand why the pastor was overlooking his God-given talents and using him to do a job that anyone could perform. Then one day as he was cleaning he found that in his heart he was worshipping the Lord. It dawned on him that what he was doing he could do to the glory of God – it was worship. It was in that place that he learned the true heart of worship. It was also in that place that he learned that it wasn't about being up on a stage. It was about serving people.

If we want to keep humble we need to learn how to serve. How good are you at doing those behind-the-scenes jobs? Are you ever the one to wash up after everyone has left? Do you ever arrive early at church to help put out the chairs? Quite a challenge, but if we know what it means to serve, humility will naturally follow.

A leader by example

David must have been such an inspiring leader. He wasn't just a man of words; he practised what he preached. It was obvious for all to see that he loved and served the Lord. I am always amused by the story of David dancing before the ark, as the Israelites made their way back to Jerusalem. David was so full of joy that he couldn't help but dance with all his might before the Lord, wearing just a linen ephod (2 Samuel 6:14). It was unheard of for the King of Israel to be seen in just a linen ephod, a garment that didn't really cover all that much. I guess a modern-day equivalent might be the British prime minister or American president leaping around in their boxer shorts shouting out praise to God. Think of the headlines the next day! Imagine, then, what the people of Israel must have thought. To see their king give such a public display of worship must have spoken volumes. They might have heard David speak of his love for God, but now they could see it. It wasn't just David's words that showed how much he loved God; it was his whole lifestyle that displayed his devotion.

We have been really challenged at Soul Survivor by these words of St Francis of Assisi: 'Preach the gospel at all times and if necessary use words.' We need to proclaim the good news, but we also need to demonstrate it. With this in mind we've tried to organise outreaches into the local community, where we serve by picking up litter, painting houses or cleaning up people's gardens. It has been amazing to see all that God has done among people as we serve them in simple ways. It has been a revelation to discover that social outreach is not just evangelistic – it is also tied up with our worship. If we just proclaim our worship with our words and don't live out our worship by serving people with our lives, there is something wrong. God says through the prophet Amos:

> I hate, I despise your religious feasts; I cannot stand your assemblies. Even though you bring me burnt offerings and grain offerings, I will not accept them. Though you bring choice fellowship offerings, I will have no regard for them. Away with the noise of your songs! I will not listen to the music of your harps. But let justice roll on like a river, right-eousness like a never-failing stream! (Amos 5:21–24)

In this passage God says in the clearest possible terms that if we do not live lives of justice and concern for others, he hates our sung worship. Mother Teresa devoted most of her life to serving the destitute and dying in Calcutta. A journalist once asked her, 'Why do you do this?' Her reply was simple and yet theologically profound: 'We do it for Jesus.' When we live a life of worship, what we do on a Sunday morning at church has integrity.

Being yourself

Another thing I love about David is that he was his own man. When he was about to square up to Goliath, King Saul told him to try on his armour. However, David was swamped in the king's fighting gear, and instead opted for a sling and five stones. Not much really when it comes to state-of-the-art fighting equipment, but David wasn't going to pretend to be something he wasn't – he was going to be his own man. Graham Kendrick once said, 'If asked to sum up the art of leading worship in one simple sentence, I think I would say, be a worshipper, be a servant and be yourself.'[3] Sometimes it's very tempting to watch gifted worship leaders and crave what they have. Occasionally we even try to copy exactly what they do, hoping that as a result we'll be more effective. This of course is nonsense. God has gifted us in unique and individual ways. Unfortunately I will never have the guitar skills of Eric Clapton or the voice of Bono, but that doesn't matter, as God delights in using me the way I am.

Respect for leadership

The relationship between pastor and worship leader is sadly all too often one of conflict. There are so many misunderstandings and insecurities that surround this partnership. While pastors are usually not blameless when this relationship breaks down, I want primarily to look at this issue from the perspective of a worship leader. God calls us to honour and respect those in leadership over us, even when that is sometimes very tough. Occasionally the pastor may be too controlling, they may not give enough space for sung worship, or they may not understand us. However, this can never justify a response of disobedience or divisiveness on our part.

David modelled in an incredible way this principle of honour. Saul was full of jealousy and rage at David's success and popularity. He saw him as a huge threat and therefore wanted to wipe him out. At one point we find

David and his men hiding in a cave. To their astonishment they see Saul, unaware of their presence, walking in and relieving himself in front of them. What a wonderful opportunity to kill Saul and free themselves from having to be on the run! David managed to sneak up behind Saul's back and cut off a corner of his robe. Afterwards David was conscience-stricken and confessed to his men, saying, 'The Lord forbid that I should do such a thing to my master, the Lord's anointed' (1 Samuel 24:6). Even though Saul was in the wrong, David acknowledged he was still the King of Israel, and therefore he needed to defer to his authority.

I often travel with my pastor, Mike Pilavachi, who fancies himself as a worship leader. This sometimes makes my life interesting. On one occasion I was leading worship in San Diego, California, and during the conference we had sung the song 'Here I am to worship' to death. I had already sung the song in this the final session of worship, but as I finished the worship time Mike came up behind me and whispered in my ear, 'Sing "Here I am to worship" again.'

I groaned and whispered back, 'I don't think so. We've sung this song too many times.'

'Sing it anyway,' Mike responded.

While everyone else continued to engage with God, we had a whispered argument. I realised Mike was serious when he whispered fiercely, 'Sing it now or I'll break both your legs!' I got the impression from this that the discussion was over. We sang the song. When I finished, the congregation continued to sing the song on their own. It was obvious that the Holy Spirit was stirring something. We finished the conference with a wonderful spontaneous time of worship, much to Mike's delight.

While I still have some questions regarding his pastoral approach towards me in this instance, I reluctantly have to admit he was right. There have been times though when he has got it wrong. I would love to recount some of these by way of illustration, but as he is still my boss I think it would be wise to leave it there! The point is not whether Mike is right or wrong, but whether I choose to submit to the authority that God has given him over my life.

Whenever I travel I meet many worship leaders who are frustrated with their pastors and churches, and are desperate for change. However, we have to keep coming back to that place of honouring those in leadership and choosing to serve them. We need to be honest with those in authority over us. In the context of friendship and commitment we have a right to challenge them over different issues. Mike is my pastor, but at times I've questioned him on things and disagreed over issues. The relationship has to work two ways. Out of this understanding we choose to respect and defer to our leaders.

Beholding is becoming

When I look at these attitudes and attributes and then examine my own life, I realise how far I fall short. Knowing the state of my heart I sometimes wonder whether I should continue to lead worship. Again in this area I find the life of David so encouraging. Throughout his years he messed up in some pretty spectacular ways – affairs, an illegitimate child, murder and pride. At times he got things drastically wrong. However, when he did, he was always quick to repent and seek God's mercy. The wonderful truth is that God loves to forgive. In the light of this, I keep coming back to a verse that gives me great hope: 'And we, who with unveiled faces all reflect the Lord's glory, are being transformed into his likeness with ever-increasing glory, which comes from the Lord, who is the Spirit' (2 Corinthians 3:18).

These words are so encouraging. Yes, I mess up, and yes there are things that I need to work on, but through the cross of Jesus I am forgiven. Transformation is a process. It takes a season. The important thing is that we are on the journey. The more we gaze at him as we worship, the more like him we gradually become. Beholding is becoming.

Notes

1. Interview with Stuart Townend in *Worship Together*, September 1994.
2. Andy Park, *To Know You More* (Kingsway Publications, 2003).
3. Graham Kendrick, *Worship* (Kingsway Publications, 1984), p. 172.

3

Never Lose the Wonder

The last few years have seen amazing advances in technology. My parents got excited about black and white television and threw a party when BBC 2 was first launched. Now with satellite and cable television there are more channels and features available than they ever dreamed of. Along with this, the Internet gives us access to more information than any of us knows what to do with, and we can talk or send pictures on mobile phones to people the other side of the world.

With all the scientific and medical advances, sometimes it is hard to find anything that astounds and surprises us. Mystery and wonder have been lost. Take the sense of wonder from human beings and you make them the poorer. Looking in a dictionary, I find words that cluster around the idea of wonder include amazement, surprise, astonishment, bewilderment, admiration, awe and fascination. When we look to Jesus, when we soak in his word, these are the kinds of response that should grip our hearts. Thomas Carlyle wrote that 'wonder is the basis of worship'. As our eyes are opened to all that Jesus has done, and as these mysteries amaze us, our only response should be heartfelt worship.

When I was a little boy, one of life's highlights was when my dad would say, 'Tim, we're going to McDonald's for dinner today.' I loved it. As we'd approach the golden arches the excitement was over-whelming. We'd join the queue and I'd order the same thing every time: Big Mac, fries and chocolate milk-shake. Every mouthful was amazing and nothing else in life could compare with eating at McDonald's. Now that I've left home and have had to learn to cook for myself, I've found myself visiting McDonald's all too often. Just recently I popped in for some lunch and ordered my usual. As I was walking out it suddenly dawned on me that something dreadful had happened. I'd lost the wonder of McDonald's!

Complacency can be such a dangerous thing. If we have been Christians for a long time we can so easily fall into this. We've heard the stories thousands of times, we've sung the songs and prayed the prayers, and now nothing really surprises us. If I'm honest, often when I read the Bible my heart isn't full of wonder. As I sing to Jesus I'm not overcome by awe. The hymnwriter William Cowper wrote in 1769, 'Where is the blessedness I knew when I first saw the Lord? Where is the soul-refreshing view of Jesus and His word?' These words are often my words. Romans 12:11 says, 'Never be lacking in zeal, but keep your spiritual fervour, serving the Lord.' We have a responsibility to maintain our passion for Jesus. We need to find those places of wonder where our souls can be refreshed by who Jesus is.

G. K. Chesterton once said, 'Let your religion be less of a theory, and more of a love affair.' For this reason we need to pray for more revelation. In my life there have been times when I've become legalistic and tried to love God more by doing religious things. These haven't deepened my passion for Jesus. The only thing that will is God-given revelation of who he is.

Keeping our eyes on Jesus

It's always horrible to lose something of worth. When this happens we are sure to search high and low until we have found whatever we have lost. For a parent, the worst nightmare must be that of a child going missing. I remember, when I was about ten, coming home from school to find my mum deeply distressed. My little brother Stephen, who was about four at the time, had been missing all afternoon. My parents had looked everywhere and the police were now involved in the search. I started running around the neighbourhood calling out for Steve, desperately hoping he'd be all right. After about half an hour I came back home and was in our back garden when I saw something in the bushes and went to investigate. To my delight I found Stephen fast asleep under the bush. He'd been playing football and had kicked the ball into the bush. He obviously went to recover the ball, but for some bizarre reason decided to have a little siesta there. Immediately everything was all right. The panic and fear became a distant memory. All that mattered was that Stephen was found.

Luke's Gospel tells us the story of when Mary and Joseph lost their son Jesus:

Every year his parents went to Jerusalem for the Feast of the Passover. When he was twelve years old, they went up to the Feast, according to the custom. After the Feast was over, while his parents were returning home, the boy Jesus stayed behind in Jerusalem, but they were unaware of it. Thinking he was in their company, they travelled on for a day. Then they began looking for him among their relatives and friends. When they did not find him, they went back to Jerusalem to look for him. After three days they found him in the temple courts, sitting among the teachers, listening to them and asking them questions. Everyone who heard him was amazed at his understanding and his answers. When his parents saw him, they were astonished. His mother said to him, 'Son, why have you treated us like this? Your father and I have been anxiously searching for you.' (Luke 2:41–48)

Whenever I read this story I'm surprised at how Mary and Joseph failed to notice that Jesus wasn't with them for so long. How could they lose their twelve-year-old son? Were they bad parents? Did they not care about Jesus? It is reasonable to suppose that Mary and Joseph loved their son. So what happened? It seems that in the rush and stress of organising everyone to return home after the festival, Mary and Joseph took their eyes off Jesus. They assumed he was in their company. They had become complacent that Jesus would always be with them and had, for a while, stopped paying attention to his whereabouts. It was only after a day that they actually took stock and realised Jesus was missing. When they eventually found him, Mary was clearly relieved, as well as being pretty cross!

We can't be too harsh on Mary and Joseph. The truth is that at times we can all get complacent in our relationship with Jesus. So often I find myself rushing around from meeting to meeting. It's only when I get to the end of the day that I look back and realise that I've failed to involve Jesus in all that I've done. I haven't been mindful of him and have assumed that I'm walking in his paths. I keep on doing all the right things, but inwardly I'm not maintaining my relationship with my Saviour.

Embracing the place of wonder

Recently on a trip to Canada I had the privilege of being able to visit the Niagara Falls. Standing before this sight I was amazed by the intensity and velocity of the waterfall. Hour after hour, day after day, year after year, water never stops pouring down. Incredibly, it is estimated that approximately 600,000 gallons of water flow over the Niagara Falls every second. As I beheld this awesome view, God spoke to me about his heart to give. For too long I looked upon God as more like a well. You dig deep for water but eventually it will dry up. However, God was reminding me that there was no end to his goodness, his mercy, his power. The deeper we dig, the more we discover. Like the torrents of water that keep on flowing at Niagara Falls, God's heart is to keep on giving to his children. He is the giver of living water and those who drink this water will never thirst again (John 4:10–14).

As worshippers of Jesus we therefore need to find oases to refresh our souls. We need to keep looking at the big picture. We need revelation. Sometimes when we've lost that soul-refreshing view, the first step to recapturing it is to become desperate. That's exactly what happened when Mary and Joseph realised Jesus was missing – they became desperate. They were 'anxiously searching' for him. When we read this it can all seem quite understated. I get anxious over watching England play football, or a visit to the dentist. In the end, however, it's not such a big deal. In the biblical context the word 'anxious' means 'to be in agony, to grieve'. Jesus' parents were deeply distressed at losing him. They realised how important he was to them and kept looking until they eventually found him. When we feel that we're in a dry place, that the fire in our heart is all but embers, then it's time to get desperate. It's time to start seeking with all we have. The cry of our hearts has to be, 'There must be more!'

The first place we need to look to discover more of God is in his word. As followers of Jesus, the Scriptures must always be close to us. In the Psalms we see how David viewed God's word: 'How sweet are your words to my taste, sweeter than honey to my mouth' (Psalm 119:103); 'Your word is a lamp to my feet and a light for my path' (Psalm 119:105). David knew how precious and valuable the Scriptures are. If we want to grow in our understanding of God, we need to feast on his word, to fill our minds with his truth. Sometimes to sit down and read the Bible takes discipline. It's not always an easy book to read. But we need to delve deep and expend ourselves in studying and reading it.

I'm fairly confident that no one reading this would disagree. Many of us do not need convincing that reading the Bible is a worthwhile thing to do. The question many of us struggle with is how to read the Bible in order to maintain a sense of wonder. Without creativity, our Bible reading can become legalistic, stale and boring. Here are some suggestions for keeping it fresh.

1. Before reading the Bible ask the Holy Spirit to give you revelation. The most common prayer Paul uttered in his letters to the churches was that they would have more revelation of Jesus. Indeed Jesus said that one of the main roles of the Holy Spirit would be to take that which is about him and make it known to us (John 16:13–14). The Bible was inspired by the Holy Spirit, so it follows that it is arrogant to assume we can interpret without his help.

2. As you read the Bible turn it into prayer. Talk to Jesus about what you have just read. Ask him questions. Thank him for what he has shown you. Praying the Scriptures is a great way to make them live in your heart.

3. Be creative. Vary the way you read the Bible. Sometimes it's good to read a book of the Bible as you

would read a novel. At other times you may want to dwell and meditate on one verse, one story or one psalm. Sometimes you may want to come back day after day to one passage with the aid of a commentary, and study its meaning. It can be very rewarding to take one character in the Bible, such as Joseph, Moses or David, and discover how God dealt with them. In order to preserve this from simply becoming theory, always ask God what lessons you can learn from this character's life. Some great books have been written on many of these Bible characters that you may find helpful.

4. Why not ask a different member of your worship band to prepare a few minutes of simple thoughts on a passage of Scripture for the start of each practice?

Alongside God's word, we need to carve out time to listen and wait. In the mad rush of life, quietness and solitude are often neglected. We miss the still small voice of the Lord. It is essential to make space in our lives to reflect and ponder. We need those places beside quiet waters where our souls can be restored. I love the story of a farmer who went to work shifting hay. While working in the hay barn, he realised that he'd lost his watch. The farmer and his friends spent many hours searching for it, but after a while they gave up and went home. Watching the proceedings was a little boy. After everyone had left, he went into the barn and lay down and waited until there was complete silence. It wasn't long before the faint sound of a 'tick-tock, tick-tock' could be heard. The boy followed the sound and was able to retrieve the watch.

We need to find those times of quiet. Every day our minds and hearts are filled with the things of this world. Too often the hectic pace of our lives drowns out the still small voice of God. Learning to listen will fuel our passion for him.

Our greatest need is to encounter the living God and draw near to him. Our prayer has to be that of Asaph the psalmist: 'But as for me, it is good to be near God' (Psalm 73:28). There are many ways to do this – reading the word, times of stillness, a walk in the country or listening to a CD, for example. Whatever it takes, hunger and thirst after him, as there is always more of God to discover. Warren Wiersbe wrote:

> This is the paradox of Christian worship. We seek to see the invisible, know the unknowable, comprehend the incomprehensible, and experience the eternal. Like David we thirst after God and we're satisfied and dissatisfied at the same time. Like Moses, we cry out for his glory, all the while knowing that our mortal eyes could never behold God's glory in its fullness.[1]

Paul, in his first letter to the church in Corinth, says, 'Now we see but a poor reflection as in a mirror; then we shall see face to face. Now I know in part; then I shall know fully, even as I am fully known' (1 Corinthians 13:12). Until we stand face to face with Almighty God, we will never fully comprehend how glorious he is. For now we see in part, we catch glimpses of his glory. As worshippers we need to press on. We need to go deeper in order to go further. We need to embrace the mystery of God, so that we never lose the wonder.

Note

1. Warren Wiersbe, *Real Worship* (Baker Book House, 1986).

4

Leading Worship

I was sitting at the back of the church, minding my own business, and as I looked out and watched people worshipping, I noticed a few enthusiasts at the front waving brightly coloured flags. I remember telling myself that I would never do anything like that – it wasn't for me. Then my heart skipped a beat as I sensed God prompt me to respond to him in worship by waving a flag. To be honest I laughed it off at first, thinking it was my mind playing tricks, but gradually I came to the conviction that it was the Lord speaking. I wrestled with these thoughts for a while, pleading with God not to make me do it. All the while we were singing, 'I'll bring you more than a song, for a song in itself is not what you have required.' I knew what I had to do. Leaving my seat I walked to the front, picked up one of the less brightly coloured flags, and started to wave it. I could feel the eyes of all my friends burning into the back of my head. As I waved the flag I felt a great release and freedom to worship. My heart was stirred to worship God in a deeper way than ever before.

God taught me some important lessons that night. The first lesson was that true worship involves humbling ourselves and bowing the knee. While I deeply respect Christians who wave flags in worship, the art of flag waving has never been something that has personally grabbed me. In fact I had on more than one occasion vowed never to pick one up. I believe the Lord asked me to wave the flag to test whether I loved him enough to look foolish in front of my friends. I have sung the line 'And I'll become even more undignified than this' on so many occasions, but this time the Lord was challenging me as to whether I was prepared not just to sing about being undignified but to actually be undignified.

The second lesson was God reminding me to find out how he desires to be worshipped and then to obey. There's a challenge in Ephesians 5:10 that says, ' . . . and find out what pleases the Lord.' We need to be people who seek the Lord's will and respond obediently to it. First and foremost that involves the whole of our lives and affects the choices we make. It also involves the way we worship in a corporate setting, whether that's a church service, a youth group or a cell group. As David Peterson says in his excellent book *Engaging with God*, 'Worship of the true and living God is essentially an engagement with him on the terms that he proposes and in the way that he alone makes possible.'[1]

There is an urgent need in the church today for God-anointed worship leaders who will be sensitive to the leading of the Holy Spirit. Richard Foster says the following about worship: 'It is kindled within us only when the Spirit of God touches our human spirit. We can use all the right techniques and methods, we can have the best possible liturgy, but we have not worshipped the Lord until Spirit touches spirit.'[2]

We cannot worship until the Holy Spirit opens our eyes to see Jesus. Therefore, worship is always a response. The Bible says, 'We love because he first loved us' (1 John 4:19). Our worship needs to be Spirit-led; in fact I would go so far as to say that the Holy Spirit should be our worship leader. Therefore it is not just a case of throwing a few favourite songs together. If we're not careful, we can miss out on the Holy Spirit's plan for a meeting simply by coming to God on our own terms, not his.

Initiation v. response

There are two ways of leading worship: initiation or response. My desire as a worship leader is to lead God's people in song by responding to what he's doing. Jesus said, 'I tell you the truth, the Son can do nothing by himself; he can do only what he sees his Father doing, because whatever the Father does the Son also does' (John 5:19). This is why ultimately the Holy Spirit has to be the worship leader. Matt Redman says, 'When we see the Holy Spirit as the worship leader, we realise more than ever that we can't make worship happen.'[3] Too often, though, we try. We slip into the mindset that by playing the songs louder or faster, or using the most popular songs around, we will have an amazing time of worship. We initiate in our own strength. This, however, cannot be the model for leading worship. Worship is more than just singing songs or dancing. As we've seen, it's about a heart's response to God.

Recently I met a retired bishop from South Africa. As we talked, he told me about his plans for retirement. He said that he'd been asking God, 'What is it that you want me to do that you will bless?' For months that had been his prayer. However, through that time God spoke to him and he realised that he'd been asking the wrong question. Rather he needed to ask God, 'Lord, what is it that you are doing that I can bless?' It sounds like a similar question but is actually significantly different. Instead of racing ahead and doing what seemed best, he knew he had to wait and see what God was doing. Then all he had to do was join in with that. We need to be asking the same question as we lead worship. On this point Bob Sorge helpfully says:

> He [God] is honouring those leaders who are coming care-fully into his presence, waiting upon him to initiate toward us, and then helping the people to respond back to the Lord with their reciprocating initiative. In this model there is much less of a tendency toward hype because the Holy Spirit is seen as the one responsible for moving the people to worship – not the worship leader or musician.[4]

Most of us know the pressure to lead worship in a way that provokes a response. Maybe we throw in a song that we know will get some hands in the air. In the end though this is all hollow. The real role of a worship leader is first to respond to what God is doing, which means at times going down some rather strange routes. God's ways are higher than our ways.

I remember a time a few years ago when I was leading worship at an event in the north east of England. There were about a thousand young people packed into the tent. As I came to what I thought was the end of the worship I turned to Mike, who was leading the service, and waited for him to end in prayer and then speak. Instead he suggested we wait, as he felt there was something more to happen. We waited for a while and then started singing the simple refrain 'Praise the Lord, O my soul, praise the Lord'. After a while the band stopped, but the young people continued to sing. The band left the stage and Mike and I sat at the side and joined in with everyone. What happened next was amazing. There was a hushed silence and then someone started another song. This was followed by a time of singing in the Spirit. Then people started cheering and shouting out praise to God. Again there was a holy silence and after a while new melodies and songs started to fill the air. We had an incredible time of responding to God and the floodgates of heaven opened. God poured out his Spirit in a very powerful way. We worshipped like this for at least 45 minutes and the wonderful thing was that no one was on a stage leading it. There was no one telling people what to do next. The Holy Spirit was leading us and a thousand young people joined together in response. It was a night I'll never forget and it reminded me of the need always to lead

God's way. Sometimes that means getting out of the way and making space for God to work.

Sometimes when leading a time of worship we need to lead strongly and move quickly from song to song. We also need at times to take our foot off the accelerator and wait to see what is happening. A question we always need to be asking is, 'Lord, what are you doing?' With all the pressures of leading the band, remembering the chords and words and then of course observing how the congregation are responding, we can forget to ask. I've discovered that it's when I keep asking that, maybe a thought comes to mind. Sometimes it's a different song; sometimes it's a line to sing out. As I've tried to obey and step out in this, often something is unlocked and we encounter God in a profound way.

I would like to say that every time I step out everything kicks off wonderfully, but sadly that is not true. As the people in my church will tell you, there have been some disasters. There have been times when I've felt God has put on my heart a line to sing and I sing it out again and again, yet no one really responds. Occasionally I've gone into spontaneous times of worship and have left everyone behind because it was Tim-led rather than Spirit-led, and that doesn't seem to work as well.

A while back Mike had a word with me about not trying to force out the spontaneous. He felt that I was trying too hard and it just wasn't happening. I appreciated his honesty and input, and realised I had got it into my head that a great time of worship always has to involve spontaneity. Whether it was a song, a spontaneous line or a time of singing in tongues, I was trying to make it all happen. It was a revelation to realise that we could simply sing five songs one after the other and have a wonderful time worshipping God. We didn't always have to sing out new melodies. Knowing that helped me to relax, and since then I've felt more confident to step out, and God has been faithful in leading me as I lead others. The key thing is learning to hear the voice of the Lord and to obey. At times things will go horribly wrong, but that's all right. We get up and start again, and keep trying to follow the Lord.

Pastor v. prophet

There is a massive difference between a song leader and a worship leader. Anyone who is musical can sing a few songs. For a church to be alive in its sung worship we need Spirit-led worship leaders, not just quality musicians. There are two aspects of leading worship that we need to keep in healthy balance. We need to be both pastoral and prophetic. Most of us will naturally tend toward one or other of these characteristics, but we need to incorporate both.

First, as a pastor, a worship leader needs to be someone who looks to include others. Worship leading is not about worshipping while others watch. I've been in meetings where the worship band are having a great time. They are going for all the spontaneous and prophetic songs like there's no tomorrow, totally oblivious to the fact that no one is joining in and the congregation have all been left behind. I was once in a meeting where the worship leader led for over 50 minutes without singing one known song. He sang out different lines and worshipped lots through the music. For some it was the most amazing time of worship, but others couldn't understand what was going on and ended up leaving. We need to make worship accessible, and therefore it's important to have a pastor's heart. Throughout times of leading worship it's vital to open our eyes occasionally to observe what's going on among the congregation.

Eddie Espinosa uses a helpful analogy. He likens poor worship leading to inviting a group of friends round for a meal. When everyone arrives they see the table beautifully laid, but the only plate with food on is the host's. As everyone sits down, the host tucks into their food, describing every morsel, explaining how good it is. Throughout the meal they wax eloquent. If you were to be involved in this scenario you'd think it strange. In the same way, we can't expect people to turn up at church to be told how good God is and what wonderful things he is doing, without giving them the means to join in. Our worship must be congregational.

In Psalm 78, Asaph says of King David: 'He chose David his servant and took him from the sheep pens; from tending the sheep he brought him to be the shepherd of his people Jacob, of Israel his inheritance. And David shepherded them with integrity of heart; with skilful hands he led them' (Psalm 78:70–72). All worship leaders have that same calling. We are called to serve God's people. It's not about an opportunity to be on stage; it's not a musical hobby. It's a calling to serve.

With this in mind we also need to understand that there has to be a place for the prophetic. The danger is that in our zeal to include others we pamper to their every desire. Anyone who's led worship in a church will be familiar with the classic request scenario: ' "Shout to the Lord" is my favourite song – we couldn't sing it tonight, could we? It would mean so much to me.' They use all the right techniques to make you feel that you'd be letting them down if you weren't to use that song. But if we only ever chose the songs people wanted, or led in a way that everyone was comfortable with, pretty soon things would get very stale. Sometimes it can be uncomfortable when God moves. I've been in meetings when he has moved so powerfully that I've felt frightened. We shouldn't be surprised when this happens. He is sovereign and knows what he's doing, and at times we need to let go and trust him.

As we follow God's heart, he will lead us to push out the boundaries in the way we worship. It is important for the church to keep on being stretched. Sometimes people may struggle and resist, but change is necessary. We need to be as sensitive as we can to people's feelings but resist the temptation to be people pleasers. To be prophetic may mean at times using different musical styles; it may involve encouraging people to sing in the Spirit, to sing a new song – their own song. Initially it may be hard work, but with a lot of encouragement and prayer it could take the church so much deeper into the experience of God's presence.

Maintaining the tension between the pastoral and the prophetic is crucial. To be prophetic without being pastoral is to enter the third heaven, have a wonderful time and after an hour realise that everyone has gone home. To be a pastor without being a prophet may mean that you keep everyone together, but together you go nowhere and the worship soon becomes dry. To be prophetic and pastoral is to take a congregation together on a journey into a deeper appreciation of and response to who God is.

Notes

1. David Peterson, *Engaging with God* (IVP, 1992).
2. Richard Foster, *Celebration of Discipline* (Hodder & Stoughton, 1989), p. 199.
3. Matt Redman (ed.), *The Heart of Worship Files* (Kingsway Publications, 2003), p. 75.
4. Bob Sorge, *Glory When Heaven Invades Earth* (Oasis House, 2000), p. 48.

5

Leading a Band

The twelve apostles had quite a dilemma. Their community was growing wonderfully as God was moving. However, the Greek-speaking Jews were complaining that their widows were being overlooked in the daily distribution of food. Something had to be done fast. The apostles decided to choose seven men to deal with the problem. What qualifications should they have been looking for in what was essentially the job of a waiter? Perhaps a stint at TGI Fridays would have been the most useful. Instead the qualification that the apostles looked for was being full of the Holy Spirit and wisdom.

In those days when the number of disciples was increasing, the Grecian Jews among them complained against the Hebraic Jews because their widows were being overlooked in the daily distribution of food. So the Twelve gathered all the disciples together and said, 'It would not be right for us to neglect the ministry of the word of God in order to wait on tables. Brothers, choose seven men from among you who are known to be full of the Spirit and wisdom. We will turn this responsibility over to them and will give our attention to prayer and the ministry of the word.' (Acts 6:1–4)

If the main qualities required to serve at tables were spiritual, the principle for worship is clear. The foremost qualifications for playing in a worship team must be spiritual rather than practical.

Being involved in a worship team is very different from being involved in a rock band. As a worship band your focus is on God and leading his people. It is not about entertaining people with a few classic Christian hits. A worship leader needs to be part of a team of people who are working together, who serve one another, and who are passionate for God. It is important to be surrounded with musicians who will first be worshippers. It is also essential that band members learn to leave their egos at the door and become team players.

Because the composition of a band is essential to everything else, I want to look first at how to choose band members.

What a worship leader looks for in a band

Many worship leaders know the dilemma of having to decide whether or not someone is appropriate to be used as part of a worship team. For some churches there are so many musicians who would love to be involved that practically there is not enough room for everyone. For other churches, their year is made when someone admits after a service that they 'play a bit of drums'. In both cases, however, it's important to think and pray through each person's involvement.

Different worship leaders may have different qualities and characteristics they look for in band members. I've tried to be honest and address the things I think are key. Musical gifting is not the first qualification for playing in a worship band. In fact the best musicians sometimes make the worst worship band members.

As we have seen, a worship team by its definition must be made up of worshippers. This seems obvious, but sometimes it can be tempting to put the emphasis on the quality of musicianship, compromising the heart values. We must choose heart over skill. We are often too relaxed about who we put up on a stage. We need to learn to distinguish between gifting and calling, and should be as careful about who we release to lead worship as we are in choosing who to preach. Not everyone who loves to sing will necessarily be called to be involved in a worship team.

Character

In terms of specific character issues, I've already spent a chapter addressing heart standards. There are, however, more specific things worth thinking about. For me it's important to involve musicians whose motivation is not to impress others. This can be difficult because musicians are often trained in an environment where the emphasis is on impressing people. In worship there is no room for performance that takes any of the limelight from Jesus. If I'm thinking about using someone in a worship band, I try to observe them in church. Now I'm not talking about obsessively stalking them and tapping their phone, but spending time with them and looking to see if they enter into worship on a regular basis. How do they treat others? Do they serve in other ways already? These are all clues to a person's character. We need to be careful of course, for ultimately it is not up to us to judge, yet a certain level of discernment is required. For the sake of the church and of the individual involved, we need to be careful about who we give a platform to. We need to look for the best in people, but we also need to be wise. As Jesus said to the twelve disciples, when making these decisions we need to be 'as shrewd as snakes and as innocent as doves' (Matthew 10:16).

Commitment to church

Being involved in worship will inevitably mean being involved with a church. Worship should always be at the heart of any church, and the style and direction will be birthed from the vision of the church as a whole. It's not healthy if musicians only turn up to church when they play. It's also unhealthy if the band heads off elsewhere during the sermon, after having led the church in worship. It can present a 'them and us' attitude. It's important that the worship team is involved in the whole service and is part of the church family. It not only brings unity, but will help when leading worship to know what God is saying to the church in other ways.

Being a worship leader will involve pastoring the

people you serve in some way. Therefore I prefer to have musicians who also see their role as being pastorally aware of those around them. It makes such a difference when band members are approachable and can be involved in encouraging people within the congregation. One of the things I value in the band I'm often with is that when we've led at different events, the musicians involve themselves with the people outside of the meetings. This models something very important. It breaks down barriers and demonstrates that everyone is coming together to follow Christ. It helps blow the myth that those up front are more special than anyone else.

It's always great if those in the worship teams are also involved in serving the church in some other way, whether it's helping with the coffee rota or in a small group. At our church we have a guideline, which is in no way a set rule, to encourage people to be involved with the church for at least six months before we look to involve them up front.

At our church we will only use musicians who are firmly committed. In one case we noticed that a certain musician only attended church when he was on the worship rota. When challenged over this he said that he could only worship God when playing his instrument. At this point we realised there was a problem. We took him out for meal and expressed our concerns. In order to help him learn to worship God without his instrument, we asked him to step down temporarily from the worship team.

A commitment to the local church is critical. The

Bible is clear that Jesus is passionate about the church – his bride. His desire is to build his church (Matthew 16:18). We must therefore seek to do the same, and as those involved in worship teams, we need to be tied in to the local church. Part of our call to love God is to also love his church. This is essential if we are to lead her in worship. I have come across many worship leaders who have rendered their ministry less effective because of their critical attitude to the church.

Building a team

Being part of a worship team can be a very intimate thing. You spend lots of time together rehearsing, sound checking, chatting and leading worship. At its best, close and deep friendships are formed. When things are strong relationally, this helps the band to flow together both musically and spiritually. So much comes out of these solid friendships. If there is trust and humility within a band, this releases the worship leader to lead. It is crucial therefore to build a team and invest in one another. Band members need to be team players, both in their attitude towards one another and in the way they play musically. It can be frustrating when musicians disappear into their own little world, totally unaware of what everyone else is playing. One simple sign of a team player is sensitivity to noise levels on stage. Everyone must keep their instrument at a level that prefers the other members of the worship team. These ways of demonstrating respect and love towards one another help forge that sense of team.

If you are leading a band ensure you make time to socialise together. It's also important as a leader of a group to input into and encourage other members. Naturally those in your band will be looking to you, and a simple word of encouragement or a note of appreciation will make such a difference. An essential part of leading involves serving those in your team. If we choose to serve, love, encourage and affirm those in the group, both for who they are and for what they bring musically, we will release life. We will also develop a sense of loyalty, commitment and unity within the band. This enables the band to grow together and cope with the tough times that will inevitably come.

Taking a lead

Some worship leaders are more natural leaders than others. The natural leaders understand that confrontation is sometimes necessary. They have broad enough shoulders to face temporary unpopularity for the sake of doing what they know is right. For others, however, leading is no easy task. Speaking personally I've had to learn to take more of a lead with the band. I'm not referring to leading times of worship here, but to leading and overseeing a group of people.

I remember the first time I led worship at a Soul Survivor festival. I was nervous and in many ways daunted by the prospect. When I came to practise with the band, all of whom were fantastic musicians who had been playing for many years, I felt extremely intimidated. Not only were they all musically much more competent than I was, they were also all older. As we practised, all the mistakes that were being made were coming from me (nothing much has changed). They were great about it and very supportive, but I felt like a loser. Despite all my inadequacies and lack of experience, however, I knew I had to take a lead. Although I found it hard, I took hold of this responsibility and tried to give direction. At one point the guitarist came up with a very interesting guitar riff, which I really didn't like. Part of me wanted to overlook it, but I knew I couldn't, and as a result I suggested that maybe he work on another idea, which he graciously did.

Leadership at times involves saying some tough things. Sometimes as a worship leader you may have to challenge members of your band, whether it's over something as simple as a lack of punctuality (some say this is a defining characteristic of a musician) or a deeper attitude problem. This is never fun to do, but it is essential. If a member of the group persistently turns up late for practice, the easy way out is to let it go and hope that things change. I have discovered, however, that it is less painful to address this early on. If left, the rest of the band will either become resentful or decide to arrive late as well. What could have been a quiet word in someone's ear becomes a major situation. At other times you may have someone in the group who comes across as arrogant. For their sake, it is so much better to challenge this attitude and encourage them to work through it.

If God has called you to lead worship, you need to embrace the cost of leadership. It is often easier for musicians to respond when the worship leader exudes a certain amount of confidence and gives clear direction. It is important to explain where you are going. This involves explaining your values for worship and also the structure and musical style you wish to pursue. I have had many conversations with worship leaders who complain that some members of their team don't understand the meaning of worship. If you feel this is the case, ask yourself whether you've clearly explained to them why you do things the way you do. Share your heart, and more importantly share the Scriptures, and allow them time to catch the vision. If everyone is on the same page it will make leading so much easier.

At times you will need to give musical advice to individuals. A friend who leads worship once mentioned to the guitarist in his group that he felt he needed to try to be more creative in his playing. The guitarist took the advice on board and worked hard to improve his creativity. Sometimes I've had to be up front with musicians to encourage them to push themselves. Most of the time people have responded brilliantly and it's helped the band to improve.

It is a good policy to be honest with your worship band. As a result trust and security will grow, as everyone knows where they stand. It's so important that we learn to speak the truth in love (Ephesians 4:15), but we do need to be careful. Often when someone starts with the dreaded words 'Now, I say this in love . . .' we know we're in for a hammering. Too often people are dumped on and criticised and we call it 'speaking the truth in love'. When we challenge, correct, discipline and give input to people, it has to come from a place of love. In the context of relationship, we can say the tough things in a way that will challenge people but also affirm them.

In the same way, we as leaders need to be open to be challenged by members of the band. I've so appreciated the times when members of my worship team have pointed out to me things that I could work on, or should be aware of. Recently a singer on the worship team hesitantly pointed out to me that my vocals weren't at their strongest on the low notes. I got the distinct impression that what she was trying to say was that occasionally I wasn't even hitting the low notes. I was devastated – as any singer or worship leader would be. I couldn't decide whether to give up leading worship for good or hit the person concerned, but because it was Beth Redman I knew I'd lose any fight! As a result I took singing lessons and I'm so grateful that Beth was honest with me. If we are going to take a lead and give input to people, we also need to be open for others to input into us. It cannot be a one-way dictatorship.

Releasing creativity

Musicians are creative people. They love to experiment and push boundaries. In church, however, we too easily play it safe and settle for the musical middle ground. This can cause gifted musicians to feel that life is being squeezed out of them. I've learned that if we want our musicians to flourish we must develop avenues for their creativity.

At our church we had a series of evenings for musicians, where there was no set agenda. We put out some percussion instruments, guitars and keyboards, and then created space for people to lead one another spontaneously. At first it was hilarious as everyone stood around too shy to take a lead. After a while someone started singing out a line and people joined in. Some started to play percussion and others began to work out different melodies, and a new song started to rise up. By the end of the evening we had really met with the Lord and people were so excited by what had happened. There was a buzz around the place and it was clear that the musicians in our church felt relieved and energised by being able to express themselves more freely.

As leaders we need to release this freedom. Sometimes, because we feel threatened and insecure, we can crush other people's ideas. Speaking personally I am painfully aware that for most of the bands I play in I am the least musical. Therefore I so appreciate being pushed in terms of creative ideas. I once worked with a guitarist who was brilliant at coming up with different sounds and riffs. Some were a tad wacky, and at times I had to suggest more feasible options, but he was totally cool when his suggestions were rejected, and he kept challenging me to improve my ideas. It's a healthy thing for a band to encourage and spur one another on to keep fresh musically. Let's not allow our egos to get in the way of flourishing creativity.

As well as releasing creativity, we also need to encourage adaptability. In the style that we use at Soul Survivor, it is quite important to be flexible. Often in our meetings we'll end up using songs that were never practised, which requires the band to be able to 'wing it'. It helps you to be able to lead confidently if you know that when you start a song, the band will be able to back you up and join in. It's a good thing to encourage your musicians to learn the songs to the best of their ability, as this allows for more freedom. At times you may want to do a song in a different key. For most guitar players, it doesn't matter if it's on the second or fifth fret – with a capo it's all usually 'D' to us. However, for all the other instruments it's not that easy. It can be very liberating when the band is comfortable playing songs in different keys, but this obviously involves a fairly good level of musicianship and I'm aware that for many churches it's a relief just to have a guitarist or a keyboard player. In the end, all I'm saying is the more adaptable a musician the better.

Communication

Communication in a band is vital. So many crash landings can be avoided by some simple signals. For these signals to work, the first thing to consider is the layout of the band. It is pointless to have a set of signals if no one can see each other. There have been occasions when I've led without being able to see the drummer properly. As a result it's been very hard to lead the band musically. You will never regret taking time at the start to ensure the band is set up properly and efficiently.

There are times during a worship set when strong signals are needed. I sometimes wonder if the reason we sing some songs to death is because not all band members manage to see the stop signal at the same time. I always encourage the musicians I work with to look at me when we come to key moments, such as the end of a verse or chorus. As members of a band we all need to be observing what's going on around us.

There are many different ways you can communicate with one another. You can have great fun developing your secret signs and communication methods. The challenge for a guitarist is finding ways of making signals without using your hands, as both hands tend to be occupied when playing. When I want to end a song, I tilt my guitar and turn to look at my drummer. If the band is set up well, everyone will be able to see this. A worship leader I used to play guitar with would signal the end of a song by doing a slitting sign across his neck. Everyone knew to stop, but the signal did not enhance the sense of a worshipful atmosphere! If I want to repeat a chorus I'll lift up one of my legs, rather like a flamingo bird. It requires balance and lots of practice, but is an effective signal.

Some songs have a little tag section or a bridge, such as the 'To Your throne I'll bring devotion' part of 'Jesus, You alone'. At times you may want to go to this section. One friend of mine would turn and wink at the drummer when wanting to signal for this. However, because I travel and often play with different drummers, I haven't felt comfortable about winking at them.

At times you may, for example, want only the drums and bass to play a part of the song. Here I would signal this by quickly pointing at the drummer and bass player.

This is the cue for the rest of the band to stop playing.

These are a few examples of the signals I use. You may have your own which are much more effective. It doesn't matter how you communicate, as long as it's clear.

In the final analysis, so many of these practical issues are more easily resolved if the worship band members have a godly character. That is why, having talked about all these necessary details, I want to end by reiterating the basis upon which the apostles chose those who would wait at tables. They looked for people full of the Holy Spirit and wisdom. So must we.

6

Choosing a Song List

It's Saturday night and you're leading worship the following morning. You sit down to prepare the song list with a notepad in front of you, but try as hard as you like, your mind's a blank. Some of the songs that come to mind have been played to death, while others don't seem to fit.

It's a horrible feeling. Sometimes as a worship leader it can feel as though you spend your whole time choosing songs. The thing I've come to realise is that there is no fixed way of doing this. I've chatted with some worship leaders who get up on a stage without having a clue what songs they are going to do. They just trust that the Holy Spirit will lead them. I can't quite work out if this is the bravest thing I've ever heard of, or the most stupid. Once or twice I've tried to 'wing it' in a worship time, but usually it's fallen flat and has revealed to others that I didn't prepare anything, rather than suggested I was profoundly led by the Spirit. I've spoken to other worship leaders who

pick their songs a month in advance. They diligently prepare and labour over what songs will flow well together.

At the end of the day, different people will find different ways of pulling together a song list, and God doesn't
restrict himself to blessing any one method. Before
we look at some practical tips on song selection, we
need to remind ourselves that whenever we lead, our
first question must be, 'What is God doing?' We should
as a matter of course always consciously ask for his
inspiration rather than just presume. If I know I'm going
to be leading worship on Sunday, I find it helpful to be
thinking of songs throughout the week. Now I have to
confess here that I don't actually do this every time.
Sometimes I leave the preparation of the song list until
the last possible moment. But I've noticed that when I
carve out time to sit down and really think and pray
through a list, more inspiration seems to flow.

So when you know you are going to lead a time of
worship, take time to pray it through and ask the Lord
what he wants to do. Are there any particular songs that
might be appropriate? Is there a theme that God puts
on your heart for the worship time? Seeking God's will
and taking time to listen is vital. It may be in that place
that a moment of inspiration is released.

As well as preparing myself spiritually, I've also come
to learn that there are many practical things that need
to be considered.

Theme and direction

When sorting through songs it's often good to work on a

theme. Sometimes the danger can be that we throw together five big classic songs that have no connection with one another. So often I've been in times of worship where there is no link between the songs and no theme is developed. By building on a topic the worship is given some direction. It can really help people to focus and respond if there are a few songs clustered around a particular subject. We may focus on the cross, repentance, intercession, God's holiness, God's faithfulness or our joy at being a people set free. By spending time on one of these subjects, space is created to let the truth of these mysteries sink into our hearts, and we are able to respond to God in intimacy. That doesn't necessarily mean that every song in a worship set has to be on that theme, as that could make the worship session very predictable.

You might find it helpful to look at the songs you use in your church and sort them into different sections. You can then work at building up the number of songs around these themes. By taking time to think it through you can be really creative in the way songs flow together. Here are some possible examples.

1. The cross

Jesus Christ (Once again) – E
You chose the cross (Lost in wonder) – A
I will love You for the cross – Bm

2. Intercession

Salvation – E
He is the Lord (Show Your power) – E
Did you feel the mountains – B or D

3. Dedication

May the words of my mouth – C
All to Jesus I surrender – C
Over all the earth (Lord, reign in me) – C

Content and engagement

There are many types of song that we use in our times of sung worship. There are hymns that are steeped in rich theology and well-crafted poetry, which stretch our intellects to worship God. We need songs of sound biblical doctrine that put into words the eternal truths of God, but we also need simple songs of intimacy, which can be instantly picked up and sung from the heart. In 1 Corinthians 14:15 Paul writes to the church in Corinth saying, 'So what shall I do? I will pray with my spirit, but I will also pray with my mind; I will sing with my spirit, but I will also sing with my mind.'

If we only had songs of content then our worship could become merely cerebral. With these songs so much of our attention is taken up by singing the lyrics and understanding their meaning that we can struggle to engage our hearts and emotions. On the other hand, if we sang simple love songs only, our worship could perhaps become shallow. The danger is that our worship could become feelings-based rather than resting on the sure foundations of the gospel. Therefore we need both types of song, and a healthy balance between the two. Some examples of simple songs are 'I could sing of Your love', 'Let my words be few', 'Here I am to worship', or 'Hey Lord'. I've also found that it can be really fresh to include short sections of songs. Again examples might include 'O come let us adore Him', 'Our God is an awesome God', 'Be lifted up', 'Praise the Lord, O my soul' and 'Thank You for the cross' – the refrain from 'Once again'. The words from these songs give us a freedom to respond to God in our own way. As we sing 'I could sing of Your love forever', each individual may have a different specific reason for singing that line. When we sing songs with more lyrical detail, our response will always be much more focused.

Seamless flow

You know the deal: the song ends dramatically and everyone is left in wonder, love and praise. Eyes closed, we wait in expectancy for the next song of worship, yet nothing seems to be happening. After a while we can't resist opening our eyes and looking to the front to see what's going on. The worship leader is frantically going through the piles of music on their stand. They can't find the next song and the panic has spread to the rest of the band. All our attention is now on them and the flow of worship has been interrupted. Often these long pauses between songs make it hard for people to keep their mind's attention and their heart's affection on God.

It is important to spend time thinking through how songs can flow together. Having a few songs that run straight into each other and are in the same key can make such a difference. Songs that flow together in the key of 'E' include 'Here I am to worship', 'Better is one day' and 'Amazing love'. Songs like 'Consuming fire', and 'Let my words be few' can flow together in the key of 'G'. Having these links can maintain the continuity of the worship. Having said this, not all songs have to flow together. If we had one long worship medley in the key of 'E' things would get very boring. Rather, keep finding ways to link songs that will bring a freshness and help focus the worship.

Something fresh

When I sit down to prepare a song list I ask myself the question, 'What can I bring today that is fresh?' Bringing variety to our worship is so important, especially if we lead week in, week out. The church can become so familiar with certain songs in certain arrangements that people stop focusing on the freshness of the truths behind them. Finding new ways of singing the songs helps keep people engaged.

There are many ways to keep the music and worship fresh. A new song can bring new revelation, and it's helpful to have a regular injection of these. However, it is important that we don't introduce too many. People need to be familiar with the majority of songs, otherwise they will find it very hard to engage. If all the songs are new, people will be more focused on the words on the screen than anything else. They are therefore not being released to connect intimately with God.

We all know the temptation to come back from a conference with six new songs and try to introduce them all in the same meeting. We then wonder why the whole church seems to hate us! Be sensitive in how many new songs you introduce, and ensure that when you do use a new song you give it at least three or four weeks to catch on. One worship leader told me that in their church they had what they called the 3–1–1 rule. Basically the idea was that they would teach a particular new song for three consecutive Sundays. After the third Sunday, they gave it a rest for a week and then on the following Sunday used it again. After five Sundays they could tell whether or not the song was working. We need to remember that not everyone in our churches is a musician and therefore they need time to pick up new songs.

Another way we keep the worship fresh is to take an old song and give it a new arrangement. There are so many fantastic worship songs we don't seem to sing any more. It can be wonderful to incorporate these songs in a new way. At Soul Survivor we have taken some of the classic hymns and given them a new feel. For example 'Amazing Grace', 'How great Thou art' and 'All to Jesus I surrender'. Another idea is to use older choruses such as 'Jesus, we enthrone You', 'Father, we love You (Glorify Your name)', 'God is so good' and 'What a wonderful Saviour (Sing Hosanna)'. These older songs can come to life again as we use them alongside all the new songs that are now being written.

Yet another suggestion is to play a song in a different key to give it a fresh feel. Sometimes we sing the same songs in the same way all the time. Familiarity breeds contempt. By taking an up-tempo song and bringing it down a few keys people can see something new. For example the song 'Thank You for the blood' is sung in 'C', which is fine when everyone is belting out the chorus. However, it would be too high to sing in a really tender way. One idea would be to take the tag section 'We'll sing of all You've done' and sing it in the key of 'A'. It would take on a more reflective feel than the upbeat declarative way we usually sing it. Another example is 'Beautiful One'. This is usually in 'D', but can be sung in a tender way by slowing it down and singing the chorus in 'C' instead. There are many songs that can be sung in different ways to inspire people in their worship, and it will also preserve the longevity of a song.

One final consideration

As I've led worship in my local church I've noticed seasons when a particular song has a special anointing. For a while it seems to express everything we want to say to God as individuals and as a community. When these songs come along, run with them. Don't be shy about using them.

However, the one word of warning is don't kill them. Sometimes we can rely on these songs too much, and because people have responded well in the past, we keep on using them. They can be a bit like a comfort blanket and we feel confident that the worship will go well if we sing that particular song. Too often I've overplayed songs and the church has grown tired of them. It's very helpful to keep a check on what songs are being used and how often they are sung. If a song is being relied on too much, perhaps you need to discipline yourself not to use it for a month. In the long run, you'll preserve the life of the song. You will also be forced to think more creatively in song selection!

7

Musical Dynamics

Next to the Word of God, music deserves the highest praise. She is a mistress and governess of those human emotions which control men or more often overtake them. Whether you wish to comfort the sad, to subdue frivolity, to encourage the despairing, to humble the proud, to calm the passionate or to appease those full of hate . . . what more effective means than music could you find? (Martin Luther)

Music can stir our emotions like nothing else. It is the universal language of love. There is great power in music. I was amused recently to hear about a school in America where the students had locked themselves in their classroom to protest over something. The authorities tried everything to remove them and in the end chose to play the Backstreet Boys (an American boy band) over and over again at a very high volume. It wasn't long before the students cracked and opened the doors, pleading for the music to be turned off!

The Scriptures, and in particular the Psalms, are full of God's people responding to him in song. In Ephesians 5:19–20, Paul encourages the church to 'Speak to one another with psalms, hymns and spiritual songs. Sing and make music in your heart to the Lord, always giving thanks to God the Father for everything, in the name of our Lord Jesus Christ.' Then in Revelation we have the vivid picture of the worship that surrounds the throne-room of heaven. Living creatures, elders and thousands upon thousands of angels encircle the throne singing the songs of heaven: 'Worthy is the Lamb, who was slain, to receive power and wealth and wisdom and strength and honour and glory and praise' (5:12). These and many other passages underline that music is an important vehicle for worship. I don't think it's stretching a point to suggest that music was created specifically for the worship of God.

Not only do we sing to God, but amazingly we see that God sings over us. Zephaniah 3:17 tells us that God rejoices over us with singing. The almighty powerful God singing over us – that must be quite some song! The gift of music helps us in our expression of worship. We obviously need to be careful not to manipulate people through music or allow it to cloud our focus on God, but there is a responsibility for us to use music to the best of our ability to glorify him.

If the lyrics of a song are like the sketches and outlines of a drawing, it's the music that brings the splash of colour and texture. How do we arrange the music in order to make our worship the most effective it can be? There is a temptation to feel that our job is done once we've prepared a list of songs. We have also seen that just as much care needs to be taken in how we plan the arrangement of the songs so that they flow together. My pastor, Mike Pilavachi, once wrote a letter to the worship leaders at our church addressing some concerns he had. Below is part of the letter:

> Do not only prepare your choice of songs but also how you will lead them. Never repeat a song for no reason. We are singing songs for too long at the moment. It is boring and pointless. If you are going to repeat a song then think what you meant to emphasise the second time. You can change the emphasis by changing the instrumentation. To repeat a song with the same musical backing, tempo and vocal emphasis is just laziness. Don't do it any more.

Being Greek, Mike is prone to making the point somewhat strongly, but he is right. It's not enough just to bash through the songs together. In this chapter, I want to look at musical dynamics and the importance of learning to play as a band.

Less is more

The sign of a truly great musician is not what they play but what they don't play. An essential component of music is space. I've had the privilege of playing with some amazing professional musicians, and the thing that has always struck me is how simple they keep their playing. They don't overplay with fancy fills or riffs. They work at getting the best sound and arrangement that will fit the song perfectly. When you hear these different parts come together you realise how gifted and able they are.

Often in church bands, musicians come together but play as individuals rather than as a band. People are usually used to playing at home on their own in their personal worship. In this context you play as much as you can to fill out the sound. However, when five of you are playing together you don't need to play as much. When musicians overplay you are left with a messy wall of sound. By the end of the second song people start reaching for ear plugs.

If you have a band that is comprised of five members – drums, bass, electric guitar, keyboards and a singer – then those five make a whole. To play as a whole, each musician should be aiming to contribute about a fifth of the music. If the keyboards are played too much, there is less space for the electric guitar to make a difference. If the drummer plays too many fills, there is less space for the band to breathe. We need to drill into our bands that 'less is more'. This involves each band member having the discipline not to overplay.

This is especially important for solo instruments, such as saxophones, flutes, electric guitars, violins and bagpipes. Because these instruments cut through the sound of a band so strongly, they are often the most easily and instantly noticed. Recently I worked with a saxophonist, and to be honest I was initially wary. I'd stood in church too many times hearing a saxophone play way too many notes. In the end you wanted to get a sniper gun and pop them off. When we came to practise I noticed how little he played. For many of the verses he wouldn't play a note, then at just the right time he'd start play-ing. The way it helped to lift the song and bring some-thing fresh to the band was wonderful. The beauty of the sounds inspired people to worship.

Song arrangements

In order to play well as a band it's important to be aware of the different aspects that make up a song. This is something I've had to work at learning. I am a gui-tarist who can only hack out chords; I can't read music and have had no musical training. When rehearsing with a band I could tell if it wasn't sounding right, but I battled to know why. This became very frustrating, as I didn't have the vocabulary to explain to the members of the band what needed to change. It took a long time to come to the arrangement that I had in my head. Identifying the different components of arranging a song helps us to discover what is or isn't working.

Groove

The groove is the rhythm section of a song. This is always the foundation upon which the melody and har-mony are built. Every song we play has a groove, which ultimately determines the feel. The groove will govern whether a song is upbeat, tense or sombre. In a band setting the groove will be dictated by the drums and bass. The drummer and bass player need to be able to hear each other and lock in together. The song will sound very strange if the drummer and bass player are playing conflicting grooves. Different grooves can be used for the same song, such as rock, country, disco, jazz or reggae. However, you will find that usually a particular song will have a groove that works best. For example a country groove fits perfectly for 'The Happy Song (Oh I could sing unending songs)'. It would be disastrous if this groove was used for 'We're going to sing like the saved'. You will probably also find that a reggae beat won't work well with 'Undignified'!

Harmony

The harmony is the chords you use for the song. The melody of a song is always set, but by using different chords beneath it, the feel of the song can be altered. The chords we use in our songs, whether they are major chords or minors, can make a large difference. For example 'The Happy Song' would take on a very different vibe if it were played with minor chords instead of the positive major chords it uses. More subtle changes can be made by slightly varying the type of chord used or the order in which they are usually played. For example there are many different ways of playing a 'G' chord which bring subtle variations.

Bass pedalling is another technique that can be effective. This can add variety to the harmony of a song. Here the bass player holds the same note while the rest of the band play the usual chords. This builds up tension and suspense that is immediately released when the bass player returns to playing the normal chords. An example of where this works well is with the song 'Lord, reign in me'. Either in the verse or the chorus, the bass would keep holding on the 'C' until it reaches the 'Am7' chord, where it would return to the normal chords. This helps add variety to the song.

Motif

A motif is a musical idea, often a melody that becomes firmly linked with a particular song. These musical ideas sit alongside the melody and help give the song a hook and something that makes it unique. Some examples of songs that have strong motifs would be 'I've found Jesus', 'The cross has said it all' and 'Lord of the dance'. Sometimes I've used these songs and tried out different motifs for a change. Each time, however, I've noticed that the song doesn't seem to work as well with the congregation. This is because the song loses a large part of its identity and sounds flat. Within congregational worship, we need catchy and singable songs that are accessible. Finding a strong motif can help people to recognise a song and, more importantly, remember a song. This frees people to focus on God rather than for ever trying to learn the tune.

A motif can also help express something of the heart behind a song. When working on arranging a song, look at what the song is trying to communicate, then try and find musical ways to convey that. This may involve an electric guitar riff or a simple piano part. Whatever it is, keep playing around until it really fits the song. A haunting melody played over an intro for a song can be a wonderful way to focus our worship on God. It may also express those emotions that are too deep for words.

Dynamics

One of the main ways to avoid the dreaded wall of sound is to work on the dynamics of a song. If you listen to any kind of music, whether it's dance, rock or classical, great attention is given to the dynamics. If the intensity of the music always stays at the same level, it becomes very boring. Without dynamics you miss the highs of a chorus or the stillness of the intimacy. There are two different ways we can work on the dynamics within our bands.

1. *Linear dynamics.* Here the dynamics of a band can be increased or decreased simply by playing your instrument louder or softer. This becomes extremely effective when everyone really builds the music together. An example of when I've used linear dynamics is in the song 'Here I am to worship'. Usually in the tag section ('I'll never know how much it cost') the band drop right down and play very softly. As we repeat this line and approach the chorus, the band start building and the intensity increases. Eventually this build reaches a climax and we explode into another chorus. This not only works well musically, but also fits with the words being sung. When the lyrics and music join together, they facilitate a wonderful expression of worship.

2. *Terraced dynamics.* This sounds pretty flashy, and you'll be able to impress your friends with this phrase, but actually terraced dynamics is very simple. Here you change the dynamics by either adding or subtracting instrumentation. The intensity of the music is increased

by adding another sound to the already existing music. The reverse is that the intensity is reduced by stripping instruments away. Again, listening to any great song you'll find these dynamics in effect. Dance music relies on terraced dynamics. Throughout a song different beats, loops and melodic riffs are interjected and taken out to help take the song on a journey. An example of a worship song that uses terraced dynamics is 'Jesus, You alone'. After the upbeat chorus we often drop back to the bridge ('To Your throne I'll bring devotion'). The final time we come to the bridge we change the arrangement using terraced dynamics. For the first line only the drums play. Then for the second line ('May it be the sweetest sound') the bass joins the drums. For the final line ('Lord, this heart is reaching for You now') the guitars and keyboards join in and build back into a final chorus. We regularly use this technique in our times of worship. Often we might have a chorus with just the bass and drums. This allows for a more percussive feel and brings a sense of freedom and space. All this helps create musical interest and helps the song flow.[1]

Musical variety

Throughout a time of sung worship it's crucial to vary the types of song used. One thing I've observed is that a lot of the songs we use fall into the mid-tempo 'power ballad' category – songs like 'Shout to the Lord', 'Here I am to worship', 'I could sing of Your love' and 'Let my words be few'. These are often the most singable songs and work extremely well. However, if all the songs are stuck in this place our music will become very boring and predictable. People end up feeling as if they're dragging their feet through mud.

Because God is so awesome and mysterious there are many different ways to describe him. It follows that there should be as many different musical expressions as lyrical expressions if we are to attempt to do justice to the wonder of God. So when playing songs of praise or songs of celebration, let's go for it and give it all we've got. Let's play these songs loud and fast, and capture all the energy we can. As lovers of Jesus we should be able to express what it is like to be full of joy as we consider all that he's done for us. Psalm 100:4 says, 'Enter his gates with thanksgiving and his courts with praise.' We need the songs that capture this exuberance and release the dancers to dance.

At the other end of the spectrum are the songs of intimacy. We can be very lazy with the way we arrange these tender songs. Usually we just play them more quietly than the rest. This leaves them sounding more boring than the other songs, and therefore harder to engage with. We need to work out parts and motifs for these songs with the same commitment that we show to the faster songs. Sometimes it can be wonderful to strip the band right back. The band do not need to play all the time – in fact they should never play all the time. A piano on its own is a very beautiful sound. There's a vulnerability and intimacy that is expressed when just the notes of a piano resound. This is lost when the whole band join in. It's important to have some songs that are played through with only a guitar or piano.

Adding some light percussion or a cello gives people space and time to focus on God's beauty.

Finally, consider using different types of instrument. Different instruments bring contrasting sounds and moods to the music. We've discovered that a real freshness can be unlocked in our times of worship by varying the instruments. Sometimes we've used lots of percussionists as part of the band. Naturally this brings a more rhythmic feel to the worship. At Soul Survivor we've discovered that this has helped us to intercede in worship. The beat of the drums gives an expression to our passion to cry out for the lost.

Another thing we've tried is a little brass section. Some arrangements were worked out which helped give some older songs a new lease of life. You may want to try a vocal group (e.g. ten singers), an acoustic band or a string section. Basically you'll have to work with the resources you have available, but whatever you have, the key is allowing for variety.

Working on different arrangements to a variety of songs helps the church to respond to the breadth of who God is. It also keeps things from becoming predictable and stale. If churches regularly sing songs in the same way at the same pace, it's no wonder people get bored with singing. Variety in the music can encourage and draw people into worship through song.

Note

1. Much of this teaching is inspired by a seminar given by Matt Weeks in Watford, 2001.

8

Practical Tips

The first time I led worship I was a gibbering wreck. It was a hot summer's evening and I'd made the bold decision to wear shorts. I turned up at church assuming it would be like worshipping on my own in the comfort of my room – there'd just be a few hundred people joining me. How wrong I was. I was shocked at all the things I had to remember: getting the music and song lists to the band, getting the overheads ready for the words, explaining to the band how I wanted the songs arranged – the list went on. It was so different from anything I had done before and was quite overwhelming.

When it came to the start of the service I was terrified. As I led in song my legs were wobbling like jelly. My main thoughts and energies throughout the time we were singing were spent on keeping my knees from knocking together. It was quite an ordeal, but I got through it. I realised that there are so many practical considerations that need to be thought through in preparation to lead. In this chapter I want to offer some practical tips to help the worship run smoothly. And the first practical pointer I want to share is don't wear shorts the first time you lead worship!

Musicians are generally people with great flair and creativity. They are not as well known for their common sense. They love to go for the moment, which at times can lead a congregation into a time of wonder, love and praise. Sometimes, however, it can lead a church into a place of mayhem and confusion. The congregation is left to wonder what on earth the musicians are up to. I've been learning that as worship leaders and musicians we need to be Spirit-led, but we also need to use our heads.

Rehearsals

'Rehearsal' sometimes feels like a bit of a dirty word. If we want to be led by the Spirit and genuinely creative, why bother practising? Surely we are just manipulating people and doing things in our own strength. I've discovered that the reverse is actually true. It is easier to be Spirit-led and spontaneous when the band has rehearsed diligently. Sometimes band rehearsals are thrown together at the last minute without much thought. This can make them boring and frustrating, as people feel they are wasting their time. One of the most important things you can do as a musical director is make band practices as effective and productive as possible.

The place to start is to make sure there are solid time boundaries. It's important that people know when they are going to start and when they will finish. If people turn up at 8.00 pm they will probably expect to finish by 10.00 pm. If, however, the practice keeps on going until 11.15 pm they will be more reluctant to turn up next time. Also, if you're going to start at 8.00 pm, make sure everything is set up and ready. It's really annoying to turn up on time and then wait until 8.45 pm before everyone is ready to begin. Either the drummer is late or there is no sound gear set up. People will feel valued and motivated if rehearsals start promptly and end on time.

As worship leaders it is our responsibility to make sure everything is ready for practices. Think about the sound gear – is there anyone there to run it? Make sure every-one is clear about what time they need to arrive. Remember that some musicians will take longer to set up. If the guitarist needs time to sort out their amp and pedals, then suggest they turn up a few moments earlier. Most importantly, make sure you are there on time. It's always embarrassing when the band is waiting around for you to turn up. Sadly I know from experience!

Generally I think about two hours is a good length of time to rehearse. It's helpful to have an idea of what you want to achieve in the practice. If you want to teach a couple of new songs, make sure you have all the music ready. It's also helpful and a good discipline to spend some time chatting and praying together. Doing this first helps people to focus their attention on God. Use this time to pray for and encourage any in the band who are struggling.

Finally, don't forget to have fun during practices. It should be an enjoyable time, coming together and being creative. The guys I work with will often try and do really random versions of songs, usually involving reggae music. Sometimes as leaders we can get so focused on the job in hand that we don't allow people to relax a bit and have fun. To get the best out of people we need to have a laugh as well as work hard at what we do.

The dreaded sound check

One of the unavoidable stresses of leading worship is the sound check. It's boring and time consuming and therefore the temptation is to cut corners. However, if the band sounds horrendous due to poor sound levels, it is hugely distracting for a congregation. If the electric guitar is painfully loud, most people's focus is on protecting their ears.

There are some simple practical things we can do to enable sound checks to go more smoothly. Again it's important that the entire band turns up on time. The sound engineer's job is made impossible if some members of the band are missing. Perhaps the thing that causes most tension during sound checks is when the drum levels are being checked and the rest of the band join in as well. It always amuses me that once musicians have their instruments in hand, they cannot resist the temptation to play. The sound engineer often has to ask people several times to be quiet as they check the levels of each instrument. Depending on the personality of your sound engineer, they may either ask you to be quiet politely, or more often than not tell you in a slightly more colourful way. It speeds things up so much if people are quiet when someone else is being sound checked.

Another item on the check list is to ensure that everyone can hear enough in the monitors. It is important that they can hear themselves, but it's also vital that they can hear one another in order to be able to play as a unit. They particularly need to hear the lead vocal and instrument to be able to follow the worship leader. If you play guitar and lead, make sure you can clearly hear your vocal and also your guitar. When singing it will be hard to get the pitch and tuning right if you can't hear the lead instrument well. On that note, it's always crucial to make sure everyone in the band is in tune. I got the hint from a worship leader I used to serve when he presented me with a tuner. There are better ways to start a worship time than with the strum of a horribly out-of-tune guitar.

A lot of tension can be avoided when the people are sensitive to one another. This is a time when musicians can prefer and honour each other. For example if the sound engineer says that the electric guitar is too loud, don't do the classic of turning it down for half a song and then cranking it right back up. Also, if you have two backing vocals, make sure that both singers can hear themselves. At the end of the day we need to serve one another patiently in the way we sound check and play together. By going in with the right attitude and heart a lot of frustration can be avoided.

Handling mistakes

If you've led worship more than once, you will have been involved in some sort of musical train crash. They're never pretty but always good for promoting humility. I was once leading worship at a youth conference and tried to flow from one song straight into 'Jesus, we enthrone You'. For some bizarre reason I couldn't find the key. I tried once, twice, even three times. Each time was more out of key than the first. Eventually someone on the front row with an exceptionally loud voice intervened and took over. Miraculously they found the right key. After a while I joined in and took it from there. There are many other horrific musical moments that have plagued my life as a worship leader. Mistakes are inevitable and the big test is how you deal with them.

One heart-stopping moment for a worship leader is when they start a song in the wrong key. Recently I started singing 'Better is one day' in the key of 'A' rather than 'E'. I started singing the chorus and soon realised that singing it this high, it wouldn't be too long before all the dogs in the neighbourhood would be running to our church to join in. There was the initial moment of panic as I realised what I'd done, then I knew I had two options. I could stop mid song and let the congregation have a good laugh at my expense. I wasn't keen on that one. Also that would totally disrupt the flow of worship. The second option was to boldly see out the end of the chorus, stop and then carry on in the correct key. I chose this option, and to be honest I think I got away with it. It was a minor incident rather than the major catastrophe it could have been.

Often mistakes are obvious to us as musicians while for many in the congregation they pass by unnoticed. Beginning a song too fast is another common mistake. I've literally had to rap verses to songs because they've been started too fast. I would encourage you to try and see out the verse and then either slow things down for the chorus or stop and restart at the correct speed. This option seems better than stopping mid flow.

Sometimes there will be mistakes that cause that dreaded train crash. A friend was leading worship and wanted the drummer to click the whole band in for the first song. Everyone had written down the song list, including the drummer, but as he was keen to preserve paper he wrote down the list on the other side of a piece of paper from the previous night's list. When he came to click in he was looking at the wrong list. He clicked into one song, while the band started another. The two songs clashed hideously and there was no alternative but to stop, laugh nervously and then start again. Sometimes this will happen, and when it does it's important not to make too big a deal out of the mistake. Don't ignore it, but don't spend the next five minutes dwelling on it and trying to justify to the congregation what happened.

If you are a guitarist, try and borrow a second guitar to have as a spare. I always make sure I have a spare guitar with me. If a string goes, as it often does with me, I just wait until the end of the song and then quickly change guitar. No big deal. As a worship leader, be prepared. The better organised you are, the fewer mistakes will occur and you'll be more equipped to handle them if they do.

Simple things like making sure the band have a correct list of songs with all the right keys make such a difference. Before each service I always chase up my band to ensure they've written down a song list. Also check you have the music you need. If you are not confident about remembering song lyrics, have the words in front of you. It confuses the congregation when the worship leader sings one set of words while they sing another. One of my most embarrassing moments came when I was singing the song 'Here I am once again'. During the chorus, instead of singing, 'I'm longing to pour out my heart to say that *You're* wonderful,' by mistake I sang, 'I'm longing to pour out my heart to say that *I'm* wonderful.' I'm surprised I didn't get stoned for heresy. It's important to ensure that the correct words are sung.

One final factor that seems to get neglected time and time again is the overhead acetates or multimedia projection. If the correct words aren't on the screen, most of the church won't be able to join in. Make sure whoever is doing the words has a list. I'll always check and double check that the operators have a correct list and order. Also, if I'm thinking of starting a song at the chorus, I'll relay this information to them. It helps to keep things flowing. It is very helpful to regard the people who are responsible for the projection of the songs as part of the worship team. Invest in them and encourage them so that they are as proficient as possible. To find someone at the last minute to do this is asking for trouble. At our church we have a team of people who know the songs well so that they can flow with the worship leader. They even have training nights. This may sound excessive, but I can't tell you what an amazing difference it makes to the worship.

Play to your strengths

Obviously bands will have varying strengths and weaknesses. Therefore play to the band's strengths. For example, when working with a less experienced drummer, it is unwise to ask them to click songs in. If their timing is suspect you will find yourself with all sorts of problems. Instead begin the song yourself and encourage them to join in when the tempo is firmly set. The same principle applies with backing vocals. A while back I led worship without any female backing vocalists. Without thinking I sang two songs with male/female echoes. If you haven't got singers, don't do male/female repeats.

If there are some musicians in the band who are less competent but are growing in their musicality, then maybe initially keep their sound levels a little lower. When I was first involved in my church's worship group I played backing guitar. Being young and naïve I played along thinking that my rhythm guitar was making all the difference to the worship. One Sunday the worship leader asked me to run up to the sound desk to give the sound engineer a message. At the desk I could see all the levels. When I looked, I saw that my guitar was turned to –20. I wasn't even coming through the p.a. system. Looking back I'm so glad the worship leader involved me and allowed me to grow without offending the church with my out-of-time and out-of-tune guitar playing. If you have a singer or musician who is less confident, don't expect them to do solos or start songs. Ease them in gently.

In this chapter I have stated the blindingly obvious, but it is often the blindingly obvious that we neglect. All too often worship leaders do the difficult things well and the simple things badly. By getting the little things right, the flow of worship in a church can be greatly enhanced.

9

Small Group Worship

There is a dynamic that is unique to worshipping in a small group. When everyone is huddled into a small lounge with just a guitar, it can be a very intimate experience. Some of my most treasured moments of worship have happened in this stripped down and simple setting. The stresses and distractions of leading a band that is leading a couple of hundred people, and remembering to sort out all the words, are removed. It's just a group of friends pouring their hearts out to their Saviour. In this situation, if the worship is led well it's amazing. If it's not, it can be pretty painful.

When leading worship in a small group it's crucial to help people focus on who it is we come before. There is a more social and laid-back feel to a small group, which is wonderful, but the down side can be that people aren't necessarily prepared to come before the Lord. The first thing on their minds is whether they will get a seat on the comfy sofa, or have to settle for the hard floor. Matt Redman says, 'In the down-to-earth setting of a home group, it's so important that we remember to prepare our hearts for a "spiritual" event.'[1] In the way we welcome people, the way we begin the worship and in the songs we sing, we need to remind people of who it is we worship. We also need to encourage people to wait for the Lord expectantly. They are more likely to come to a larger church setting ready to meet with God. There is often a greater sense of expectancy and excitement that God will work powerfully. However, when the big band and p.a. system are not there and it's just simple little you on an old Yamaha guitar, the expectancy levels are at a bit of a low. Jesus said, however, that when two or three people come together in his name, he is there with them (Matthew 18:20). Seeing and recognising this truth raises faith levels that we can significantly encounter God in the small group context.

Embrace the intimacy of a small group

Perhaps where worship tends to nose dive most in small groups is when we try to replicate what happens at church during a main Sunday service. It would be weird to gather a cell group of eight people and then cram into the room a drum kit, a bass and electric guitar, and keyboards. The word 'overkill' comes to mind. When preparing to lead worship in a small group, embrace the uniqueness of the setting. There's space for more spontaneity, as the atmosphere is more relaxed. One of the key things is to help people feel comfortable. There can be a very exposed feeling about this setting. With only ten or so people, everyone can hear each other sing. For some that's quite daunting. Not everyone can sing in tune, and to sing in front of a few people is really intimidating.

When leading in this context it's important to sing out loudly and boldly. If you set the tone and are confident, others will have a clear lead to follow. If they can't hear you, don't be surprised if some opt out and choose not to sing. It helps enormously if you strum your guitar confidently and in time. In a small group setting a song can often drag. It's good to work at strumming in time and well. If you're starting out and have only been playing the guitar for a short while, you might find it helpful to buy a metronome. You can then strum along in perfect time, as it will show you if you are speeding up or slowing down. Another option is playing along to a CD. Whatever you do, dedicate yourself to working at improving your playing. In a small group where there is no band to hide behind, it becomes obvious whether or not you can play confidently and in time.

Choice of songs

In this setting some songs will work better than others. For example, although I've never tried it, I don't think 'I will dance, I will sing' will go down quite as well in a cell group as it does at a festival with a few thousand. I'm guessing that a conga probably won't kick off! People might feel a bit more reserved. It's a great idea to try and build up a repertoire of songs that work well. Here are some types of song that are best avoided in a cell group setting.

Too high

When singing 'Shout to the Lord' with a thousand people, it seems so easy to nail every note of the chorus. However, when sung with only ten people, some will struggle. A lot of the songs we sing are quite high in the chorus. It's vital to keep a repertoire of songs that are in comfortable keys. If they're too high you can forget it, as many will choose not to sing. Some might try, but as soon as their voice cracks, they will first go red and then keep quiet. I've found that it helps to take some of the songs and sing them in a lower key. For example, 'He is the Lord (Show Your power)' is usually sung in 'G'. In a cell group I would sing it in the lower key of 'E'. In fact a lot of the songs that are in 'G' I would often drop to 'E'. Two examples are 'Consuming Fire' and 'Let my words be few'. Keep the range comfortable for people.

Male/female echoes

It seems to me that most women in the church can sing beautifully, but if we're honest, some of us guys struggle a bit. If there are two guys in your cell group and nine ladies, don't be cruel to the men in the minority. Don't sing songs with male/female echoes. There's nothing more embarrassing than two guys singing badly out of tune, while the ladies echo with angelic tones. Again it comes down to thinking about who's in the group and how you can free them to really worship. If you have a group of strong singers, you can get away with male/female repeats. If you don't, you can't.

Too wordy

Most front rooms probably won't be equipped with a state-of-the-art PowerPoint system. Often people have to learn songs off by heart and there's no way they'll be able to memorise long and complicated lyrics. Unless you use song sheets, the more wordy songs seem to work less well in a small group context. The songs that work best are simple and singable ones that can be learned really quickly. People will feel more confident if they know the song, or can see that the song is easy to pick up. It's also wise not to introduce too many new songs. If you are going to introduce new songs to a small group, make sure you sing them regularly over a couple of months, so people can become familiar with them.

I've found that using sections of songs is very effective in a small group. There is more on this in Chapter 6, 'Choosing a Song List'. Singing a simple chorus or the tag of a song gives flexibility and takes away the pressure of having to memorise many different songs.

Embrace the freedom of a small group

The beauty of a small group is that there is time and space to be creative. Sometimes when leading with a band, it's harder to flow from song to song, or hang around on a particular chord sequence, as this has to be communicated to the rest of the band. In a small group there's also more space for everyone to enter in and contribute. Paul says in 1 Corinthians 14:26: 'When you come together, everyone has a hymn, or a word of instruction, a revelation, a tongue or an interpretation. All of these must be done for the strengthening of the church.'

In this context there is a greater freedom for people to contribute. If during a church service the entire congregation started singing their own songs and everyone shared their blessed thoughts, things would soon get out of control. A small group is a safer place to explore this spontaneity. I always try to encourage people to start a song if they feel it's appropriate. At times it might be good to allow space and just wait. People may want to pray for a while or read out some scriptures. It's great to let things flow. If the group really gels and people trust one another, they can be encouraged to step out more.

One year the staff at Soul Survivor Ministries met for a short retreat down in Somerset. On one of the evenings a friend of ours came to lead some worship, and he brought something really fresh to us. Rather than singing the usual six songs, he opened up a psalm. He then played three simple chords over and over. As we read through this psalm and let its truth speak to us, he encouraged us to sing out different lines from the psalm. He began and sang out a line or two. Then he allowed space for others to contribute. It was a wonderful evening as we worshipped God from the Scriptures. The key is to find a simple melody that people can catch on to. Throughout the evening we made some mistakes: some of the melodies didn't scan and occasionally the tune was 'alternative'. However, this didn't matter and we carried on worshipping. There was a freedom and creativity that was inspiring.

The small group context can be the hardest setting in which to lead worship. It is the place where everyone is most vulnerable, due to the smallness of the gathering, and where you the worship leader are the most vulnerable, as there is no band to fall back on. For this reason it is also the best place to start. There can be no finer training ground.

Note

1. Matt Redman (ed.), *The Heart of Worship Files* (Kingsway Publications, 2003), p. 105.

10

The Art of Crafting

When the artist Sting was asked how he wrote his songs, he responded, 'I have to say I really don't know. A melody is always a gift from somewhere else; you just pray that you will be blessed again.' I love that. It acknowledges the fact that there is a mystery to writing melodies. In all the years I've been involved in trying to write songs, I've never come across a set formula. How I wish there could be an easy A, B, C format to writing great songs. It would make the life of a songwriter much less painful.

At times I find writing songs extremely frustrating. It involves both pleasure and pain. To stumble across a melody and a lyric that mould together is wonderful. However, to get to that place involves the hard graft of working and then reworking ideas. Often when I'm playing guitar in my room I'll start singing out a tune. Within minutes a song is being formed, and playing it through I'll be convinced that this is the greatest song ever written. The next day I'll come to play the song again and it will be a totally different song! The melody suddenly seems tired and boring, while the lyrics now feel predictable and cheesy. After singing a couple of choruses I'll feel rather embarrassed that such a song should exist within me. Does this ring any bells?

Someone once suggested that songwriting is 10 per cent inspiration and 90 per cent perspiration. The inspiration happens in those mysterious moments when an idea pops into your head and you have the basis of a song. The perspiration is the work that's involved to complete that song. Many of the songs I hear are great ideas, but often feel incomplete. It's amazing how songs can be improved by sheer hard work, but this involves a willingness to put in the time and effort.

In this chapter I want to delve into the art of writing congregational worship songs. This means that some of the examples I use might not be as appropriate for people who write songs to be sung in clubs and gig venues. For example, when writing a worship song, it has to have lyrics that people can understand and sing. If you're writing a song that only you and your band will play, you can be more cryptic.

Journalling songs

Inspiration can come at any moment. Part of the journey of being a songwriter involves journalling these thoughts and revelations when they come. It's always handy to have a notebook to hand to jot down thoughts, phrases and distinctive words. I often find that a sentence at church might trigger off an idea. The song 'Consuming Fire' begins with the words 'There must be more than this'. The song was birthed out of a time in our church when we were desperately seeking after God. One Sunday morning the associate pastor's wife got up to speak and kept repeating those words. They resonated within me and the song flowed out fairly quickly. Although I wrote the song, in many ways it was a song by our church. It might be that a thought is triggered when reading a book or watching a film. Quickly document it so that you can return to it later. Don't rely on your memory, as so often we forget.

One of the best things I ever did was invest in a portable mini-disc player to record song ideas. Now whenever I get an idea, wherever I am, I can quickly record it onto mini-disc. Once it's recorded, the idea is always there to return to. I have never written a complete song in one go. Often ideas come in sections. For example, when I wrote 'Here I am to worship', I initially wrote the verse and the tag section. I tried for months to write a chorus, but every idea I came up with made me cringe. After a while I gave up. About six months later I started playing around with the verse again. When listening to a tape of old ideas I stumbled across a melody that seemed to fit with the verse I had. It was a great moment when the song came together. So many of my songs are compiled in this way.

Evaluating songs

A good way to explore the practice of songwriting is to

pull songs apart. When I think I might have finished a song, there is a process I always go through to see if it's as strong as it could be. There is a series of questions I will ask myself to help assess the state of the song. When working through songs, there is a need to be ruthless. A good songwriter should never settle for second best.

Does the song help you to worship?

Songs of worship must be formed from a life of worship, and worship always begins with revelation, to which we then respond. As we set our sights on God, there will be so much to respond to. That has to be the ultimate place of inspiration. Looking through the Psalms, God is described and responded to in many ways. The poetry is heartfelt and vivid, and the songs have remained with us through thousands of years. Why is this? Is it because David and the boys knew how to pull a few heart strings and write some great songs? Did they know what the people wanted to hear? Of course not. They simply responded to what they saw.

David, as a shepherd boy, spent night after lonely night carefully tending his flock. When he wrote in Psalm 23, 'The Lord is my shepherd, I shall not be in want. He makes me lie down in green pastures, he leads me beside quiet waters, he restores my soul,' it meant something intimate to him. He understood what was involved in being a shepherd, and knew what it meant to call the Lord his shepherd. The passionate worship captured in the Psalms flowed from encounters with the living God. If we desire to write songs that will glorify God and cause his name to be praised, we too need to start in that place of encounter. As songwriters we need to consume ourselves with God, to immerse ourselves in his truth.

After I've written a song, I'll use it in my personal times of worship for a while, usually for at least a couple of months. If the song inspires me to worship, and stays feeling fresh for a while, then I start to think that it might work in a church setting. There can be a danger of forcing out songs. We sit down and rely on our expertise and skill to write a new worship song. We go through all the right motions, but our hearts become dislocated from the process. More than well-written songs the church needs Holy Spirit-inspired songs that release people to worship. These songs will only come from a hidden life of worship.

Is it theologically sound?

These are exciting days for songwriters. Songs are ministering to people and being sung all over the world. Eddie Gibbs, Professor of Church Growth at Fuller Theological Seminary, said that songwriters 'have far more ability to impact people than preachers or authors'. We need to realise that there is a responsibility that comes with this. People may sit in church and listen to sermons, but few will remember much of the content. Not many go around reciting the key points from the pastor's talk throughout the week. However, some of the songs sung in church stick in our minds throughout the rest of the week. The lyrics of these songs become deeply entrenched in us. As songwriters we therefore have the power and influence to shape people's image of God.

Imagine if someone visited your church every morning service for a month and only listened to the songs you sang. They didn't hear any preaching or liturgy or prayers – just the songs. What would this say about your church's theology and beliefs? How would it reflect the God you worship? It's quite a scary thought. Gordon Fee said, 'Show me a church's songs and I'll show you their theology.' In this light, we need to make sure that we are theologically accurate. We need to be singing truth. Our worship has to be biblical. Those who are gifted musically and lyrically are not necessarily the most able theologians. Sometimes in the attempt to be creative, lyrics are written that aren't actually scriptural. It's not that anyone is trying to be heretical – more that they've got confused. Therefore it's essential to run lyrics by someone. Before I use a song in worship, I'll always run it by my pastor. He has a good grasp on the Bible and has at times been able to point out areas where lyrically things are confusing. It's a good accountability to have.

Jesus said to his disciples, 'If you hold to my teaching, you are really my disciples. Then you will know the truth, and the truth will set you free' (John 8:31–32). The truth of God's word sets people free. It is therefore important for God's people to be singing this truth. I've been trying to fill my songs with Scripture. One tool I've found indispensable is a concordance. When writing a song, a theme obviously develops. When I've got to that place I'll open up my concordance and find as many verses on that theme as possible. For example, I wrote a song called 'Maker of all things', which was about God as Creator. When I came to complete the lyrics I looked up in a concordance words such as 'Maker', 'Creator', 'heaven', 'earth' and 'glory'. Writing all these verses down on paper, I now had pages of lyrical ideas. Different verses inspired a train of thought and helped give fresh impetus. The real skill is to then take these scriptures and unpack their meaning. Sometimes we get so comfortable with verses from the Bible that we know the words in our heads, but the meaning is lost on us. The job of a poet or lyricist is to find new ways of unpacking age-old truths.

Are the lyrics original and fresh?

There are so many classic Christian clichés. Sometimes we can be lazy and rely on the same old lyrical phrases for our songs. We've bust a gut writing a tune, and now we just want to finish the song off, but we need to ensure the lyrics stay strong throughout the whole song. Sometimes the final verse can suffer as we rush to finish the song. The challenge is to find fresh and original ways of expressing who God is. When asked what makes a good song, Brian Doerksen, a worship leader and songwriter from Canada, said, 'Songs that cross borders – borders of time, denomination and musical style – and are universal and unique. People respond to them saying, "That's exactly what I wanted to say to God, but I never thought of saying it that way." ' It's wonderful when we sing a song or a line that gives a fresh revelation of God. It helps us to see him more fully.

A worship leader and songwriter who excels in lyrics is Graham Kendrick. I've been inspired to hear how diligently he crafts and hones his lyrics. In one song he wanted to write a line about the stars praising God. To do this he read through a book on astronomy to find different terms and names for the stars. He came across a set of stars called a 'jewelled cluster' and wrote the line 'And stars in jewelled cluster say . . .'. Here's an example of someone digging deep for a fresh lyric. Personally I know I've often settled for second best. I'm working at trying to discover new words to unravel the wonders of God. Two sources that have helped me are old hymnbooks and Christian poetry. Some of the hymns contain such a breadth of who God is, and use language in a stunning way. The same with poetry. Observing a turn of phrase or a use of words has helped me try and get beyond Christian jargon.

Looking through the songs we sing, there are a lot of words we use regularly. We often sing words such as 'worthy', 'praise', 'love', 'soul', 'glory' and 'honour'. These are great words, and people in the church know what they mean, but at times I think we overuse them. I've been trying to think of new ways of saying, 'Jesus, you're worthy.' What does it mean for Jesus to be worthy? What characteristics does that involve? When I'm looking through a song I'll try and count how many times I've used some of these words – especially the 'love' word. It can be a bit embarrassing to realise how many times I've put that word in a song. Maybe set yourself a little challenge of trying to write a song without the word 'love' in it. It will force you to be more creative in describing God.

As well as being unique, we also need to be universal.

A congregational song needs to be one that everyone can sing and mean. A lot of songs come out of personal experiences and are naturally very intimate. If we're not careful we end up writing lyrics that mean everything to us, but absolutely nothing to others. I had a friend who wrote a great song about finding security and worth in Jesus. He was heavily influenced at the time by a great singer with bleached blonde hair. Part of the song looked at the pressure of trying to be like other people. He wrote, 'I can't sing like you, not for lack of trying. I don't look like you, not for lack of hair dye.' A humorous line that in many ways conveyed a lot. However, if that were to be sung in a church it would cause confusion. People would wonder about the connection between hair dye and God. It might be very powerful for the purple rinse brigade, but for most the lyric would be lost. Our lyrics need to be something that everyone can make their own and sing to God.

Is the song complete?

It is always worth waiting for a song to be complete before using it in church. To finish a song can take a while. The song 'May the words of my mouth' took me about three years to write from start to finish. I could not get a chorus I was happy with, and at times I wanted to give up. There were a couple of choruses I nearly settled for, but now I'm so glad I didn't. Perseverance is important in songwriting, and if you're not a hundred per cent sure that the song is complete then wait.

When evaluating your songs you need to go through each section (verse, bridge, chorus) and each line to see if it is as strong as it could be. If there's a line that isn't working, either scrap it or craft it until it fits well. Also ask yourself whether all the sections are in the right place. It could be that you've written a verse, a bridge and then a chorus. Maybe the song doesn't need the bridge. Would it work better with the verse leading straight into the chorus? You could always use the bridge as a tag section at the end. It might be that you have a song with a verse and a chorus. It could be worth trying to write a tag at the end. This can give a song a real climax. When writing 'I'll always love You', I initially had a verse and a chorus. I played it to a friend, who suggested that I write a tag. The tag is now my favourite part of the song.

People often ask me how I know when a song is finished. I think one of the best ways is to ask others. There are three or four people in my life who I always play my songs to. They love me enough to be brutally honest. Although at times it's annoying to hear that a song I thought was great needs a lot of work, I'm so thankful for their input. They can point out areas that need work, lyrics that are cheesy and tunes that are tuneless. The process of rewriting then begins. When I've changed things around we sit down again. We keep doing this until there's an agreement that the song is finished. Sometimes, as songwriters, we are not the best judge of our songs. When I wrote 'Here I am to worship', I didn't think it was very good. In fact I kept it on the shelf for quite a while. It wasn't until Mike heard it that he strongly encouraged me to use it. To be honest, if he hadn't heard it, I don't think I'd have used it much. Find those people who can encourage you in your songwriting but can also give you sound and constructive criticism. It will help you improve as a writer.

Is the tune singable?

There used to be a television programme called *The Old Grey Whistle Test*. This owed its name to the theory that a record would be a hit only if its tune was so memorable that old people with grey hair could remember it and whistle it. The singability of congregational worship songs is crucial. You can have the most incredible lyrics and structure, but if the melody is difficult to sing it won't catch on. With the tunes we sing, there need to be natural hooks that help people pick up the song and remember it. The songs also need to be accessible to allow people to enter into worship.

Most churches aren't heaving with professional singers. Some people in the church will be tone deaf and others will struggle to hold down a tune. If you fill your songs with falsetto notes or complex melodies, the majority will struggle to sing them. I always run my songs by Mike Pilavachi, my pastor. To put it kindly, God hasn't gifted Mike with the greatest voice in the world, but it's been fantastic to play my songs to him and get his feedback. Usually we'll try and sing them together. Often he'll point out a note or section that feels harder to sing, and most of the time I'll go away and play with some different ideas and simplify it. Obviously you don't want to end up with extremely simple and predictable melodies, but you do need to keep the congregation in mind.

The chorus of a song is particularly important. It's always a disappointment to hear a song with an amazing verse that promises so much, yet when you get to the chorus it fizzles out. Matt Redman uses a phrase I like: 'Don't bore us – get to the chorus.' A strong singable chorus can cause the worship to explode into life. I find writing choruses the hardest thing. You can't force them out – it's always important to wait until they are right.

Another consideration is the vocal range of a song. Being a bloke who can't read music, it took me a while to realise that there is a difference between the male and female voice. I couldn't understand why all the female singers at church kept complaining that the choruses of my songs were too high. I could sing them easily, so why couldn't they? I was all set to suggest that they embark on singing lessons. Now having understood some of the differences, I am more mindful of making sure songs can be sung by everyone. I have a personal rule that I won't write a melody with a note that goes above a top E, and I'm trying to discipline myself to keep it below a top D. Most people should be able to hit that note. A chorus will always fall flat if it is too high. People won't be able to reach the notes, and rather than sound like a strangled cat, they will probably give up and not sing. At the other end of the scale, I won't use a melody that goes below a bottom B♭. Here again people are likely to struggle to hit these low notes and the song may lose its effectiveness.

Avoiding writer's block

The dreaded writer's block – how do you overcome it? Creativity often ebbs and flows. At times you will have ideas flowing out of you, while at other times you won't be able to come up with a thing. That's part of the deal. There are some things that can help stimulate new ideas. If I'm feeling dry, I try to find new avenues of creativity. One way is to listen to new music. If you listen to the same type of music all the time then naturally you'll start to write in that same style. It can be very refreshing to listen to a totally different genre of music. Hearing different melodies and arrangements is a wonderful way to keep fresh.

Another thing I find helpful sometimes is to try to write a song away from my instrument. Naturally melodies are formed around the chords you play. If I'm writing a song in 'D', the chords I tend to use are A and G (or Bm if I am feeling adventurous). The same chord progressions tend to lead to the same tired melodies. If, however, you aren't restricted by an instrument your melodies are free to go wherever they seem fit. After a melody is formed you can return to your instrument and work out the chords. You might find that you've ended up using a different chord progression or time signature than you'd naturally use. This is great for trying to break away from the norm.

In the same way a freshness can be unlocked by finding new chords. Different chords bring different sounds and moods, and can spark off inspiration. You may find it helpful to buy a chord book and try different ways of playing. If you can, try and write songs on different instruments. Sadly I can only play guitar, but writing a song on an electric guitar can push you in a varied direction from using an acoustic. Sometimes it's easier to write more 'rocky' songs on an electric guitar. You may want to try using a twelve-string guitar or a high-strung guitar. If you can play different instruments, try writing on each one. See what songs come out of it.

Finally, don't give up. When I was 17 my church went away for a weekend together. On the final morning a team came to pray for my youth group. As I stood there with my eyes closed a lady pointed to me and gave me a prophetic word. She felt that I had been struggling to write songs for a while and was close to giving up. The encouragement was to keep on persevering, as God was with me. I was blown away. For a couple of years I'd been trying to write songs and was so discouraged and low about the songs I'd written that I did indeed feel like giving up. The fact that I hadn't shared this with anyone made the word even more remarkable. I left that conference floating on air. The interesting thing was that it still took me about a year after that to write a song that I felt I could use in church. I realised that the key encouragement in that word was to persevere.

We have the Holy Spirit of creativity living within us. As we wait on him, his divine inspiration will release songs of salvation and praise. As we add our own per-spiration to this inspiration, we will find that songs will eventually come to bless the Lord and bless the church.

One Last Thing . . .

In this little book I have tried to summarise some of the practical things I wish I had been told when I first started leading worship. I have also looked at some of the spiritual principles that I believe are vital for anyone who wants to lead God's people in worship. The temptation when starting out in leading worship can be to feel daunted. I have learned not to see leading worship in terms of success or failure, but more in terms of a journey, where we are constantly learning.

When I was 19, I spent a year living in Durban, South Africa, working as a youth pastor. It was an amazing year for me and God taught me some invaluable lessons, the most significant being that he uses weak and broken people. When I left England to travel out to South Africa, I was full of hope and excitement. Initially I travelled with a friend, but sadly after a few weeks he became ill and had to return home. I'll never forget that feeling of being totally alone and out of my depth. I was living in a foreign country, I had no friends or family to rely on and I now had to lead a youth group – something I had never done before. My confidence was so low that it felt as if everything had crumbled around me. About this time I stumbled across some words by William Carey. He said, 'Attempt great things for God. Expect great things from God.' In the midst of my struggles I decided to put those words into practice.

At one point early on in the year, I was organising a youth weekend away. I had diligently planned ahead and arranged a speaker to lead the weekend. Literally four days before the event, she phoned up to inform me she had to pull out. Disaster! I contacted everyone I could think of, and eventually realised I was going to have to give the talks myself. It was all very stressful, and as we drove to the camp my heart was seriously lacking in faith. I was expecting the worst. On the second night I spoke on the prodigal son (as all good youth pastors do) and as I finished, I knew that we needed to allow space for God to minister his love and forgiveness into people's hearts. I'd never led a ministry time before and I was terrified. I invited the Holy Spirit to come and then simply invited people forward if they wanted to receive prayer.

What happened next blew me away. Gradually people came to the front and God started moving in a very powerful way. Many tears were shed as young people received God's acceptance and mercy. In that night, four people made first-time commitments. Later, two girls came up and told me that they had been speaking in a funny language and didn't understand what was going on. I explained to them about the gift of tongues and how it was a wonderful gift from God. That weekend God breathed life and passion into a small youth group. I had the privilege of stepping out in weakness and watching him do what I could never do in my own strength.

Jesus said, 'You're blessed when you're at the end of your rope. With less of you there is more of God and his rule' (Matthew 5:3, *The Message*). At the end of the day this is our desire: more of Jesus. It's so liberating as a worship leader to know that our own strength or gifting is not important. Our motto must be that of John the Baptist: 'He must become greater; I must become less' (John 3:30).

These are exciting times. God is doing amazing things throughout the world to bring glory to his name. For any involved in leading worship, or playing in a band, it's time to step out. There is so much more that God is wanting to do. As we attempt great things for him, I know that God will do great things for us – things we could only ever dream of. So let's go for it!